ARNOLD ROSEN is a professor at Nassau Community College in Garden City, New York. He has taught at New York City Community College and at Hunter College. Professor Rosen has also presented seminars and is a well-known speaker and consultant on office automation, education, and training. He has served as President of the International Word Processing Association. He holds a BS degree from Ohio State University and an MS degree from Hunter College. Professor Rosen is the author of six books, including *Word Processing* (Prentice-Hall).

Arnold
Rosen

GETTING THE MOST OUT OF YOUR WORD PROCESSOR

Covers all of the functions, features, and applications of these powerful office automation tools

A SPECTRUM BOOK

Prentice-Hall, Inc., Englewood Cliffs, N.J. 07632

Library of Congress Cataloging in Publication Data

Rosen, Arnold, 1932–
    Getting the most out of your word processor.

    "A Spectrum Book."
    Bibliography: p.   Index: p.
    1. Word processing equipment.   I. Title.
HF5548.115.R668   1983   652   83-3073
ISBN 0–13–354555–5
ISBN 0–13–354548–2 (pbk.)

ISBN 0-13-354555-5

ISBN 0-13-354548-2 (PBK.)

This book is available at a special discount when ordered in bulk quantities. Contact Prentice-Hall, Inc., General Publishing Division, Special Sales, Englewood Cliffs, N.J. 07632.

A SPECTRUM BOOK

Printed in the United States of America

10   9   8   7   6   5   4   3   2   1

Prentice-Hall International, Inc., *London*
Prentice-Hall of Australia Pty. Limited, *Sydney*
Prentice-Hall of Canada, Inc., *Toronto*
Prentice-Hall of India Private Limited, *New Delhi*
Prentice-Hall of Japan, Inc., *Tokyo*
Prentice-Hall of Southeast Asia Pte. Ltd., *Singapore*
Whitehall Books Limited, Wellington, *New Zealand*
Editora Prentice-Hall Do Brasil Ltda., *Rio de Janeiro*

To my wife, Estherfay Shapiro,
and my son, Paul.
They have given me
the inspiration and love
to write this book
and represent the measure
of my happiness.

Contents

Foreword, ix

Preface, xiii

1
Introduction, 1

2
Basic Features and Functions, 23

3
Advanced Software Features, 37

4
General Applications, 51

5
Industry and Personal Applications, 67

6
Plugging into "The Office of
the Future," 87

7
Care, Maintenance, and Service, 119

8
Supplies and Accessories, 139

9
Ergonomics, 157

10
The Future, 181

Appendix, 193

Index, 201

Foreword

Thank you, Spectrum, and thank you, Arnold Rosen, for the invitation to write a foreword for *Getting the Most Out of Your Word Processor,* for this book is as timely as this morning's sunrise.

For the past three decades I have observed and participated in the revolution that has taken place in office technology—a revolution that has seen equipment evolve from an electromechanical base to a base derived from minute memory chips, a revolution that has taken the computer from the giant room-size units to small desk-top machines that are even more powerful than their huge predecessors.

I recognized quickly the profound effect that the new word processing technology would have on how information is handled. Because of this perception, I have involved our company in a wide network of word processing learning centers across the country. These centers have placed our company at the leading edge of this new technology. We intend to remain there in the future through continued innovation and development.

When the history of word processing is someday written, it will show three stages, or eras. First, there was the "How does it work?" stage, and of course schools and many offices still have this question as their primary concern. If you are yourself an operator and must switch from one machine or model to another, "How does it work?" is your whole concern.

But "How does it work?" is only a passing phase. It is now well established that any *skillful* typist who is reasonably comfortable with the *technicalities* of the English language and who *wants* to learn how to operate word processing equipment can readily do so.

So the second stage comes about, the era of "What *else* is the equipment good for?"

As work force suppliers, we naturally ask "What do you wish the temporary worker to do on your equipment?" when a client calls us. The answers indicate how rapidly word processing is changing. "To keyboard a long report" or a document or a whole book is now commonplace. "To prepare a mailing, individually addressed, to our 463 dealers," is also commonplace now. "To handle this week's secretarial correspondence" is routine and ordinary. More and more new uses are evolving, from something as esoteric as "Handle our electronic mail with our computer center in London" to something as mundane as "Revise the glossary of our former equipment to fit our new model." Yes, users of word processing equipment are learning more and more ways to use their equipment, above and beyond whatever cost-effective designs led to its purchase in the first place.

With the solution of the mystery of how the equipment works and with gratifying discoveries of what the equipment is good for, it is natural that a third area of interest would emerge, and it has: "How to get the most out of this equipment?"

And that is what this book tells.

If there is anyone in America who knows how to get the most out of word processing equipment, it must be the author of this book. Arnold Rosen is a professor of secretarial science at Nassau Community

College, on Long Island. He is past president of the International Information/Word Processing Association. He is author or coauthor of many books on the subject of word processing. He is consultant to an impressive clientele of business firms—both users and manufacturers of the equipment.

His authoritative, accurate, and enthusiastic suggestions for *Getting the Most Out of Your Word Processor* will help you realize that you are truly involved in the most exciting development in the history of the office: word processing.

The opportunity for you is now.

WILLIAM OLSTEN, C.E.O.
The Olsten Corporation
Westbury, Long Island, New York

Preface

Congratulations! As an owner of a word processor you have taken an important first step into the automated office. At first glance, the screen and the keys on your word processor may remind you of—a computer! For people who are "computer shy," the first reaction can be one of mistrust. Let's examine your new word processor more closely and see how it can help improve your office operations—especially the typing function.

Your new word processor is a magic box that makes keyboarding and creating information easy, accurate, even *fun*. To create a document, just sit down at the keyboard and type. The text is displayed on the screen as it's typed. The display gives you the opportunity to review and revise work in progress before it is printed. Mistakes? Errors? Drop a comma? Hit a wrong key? Revise a paragraph? You don't have to get out the correction fluid or fuss with correction paper anymore. Simply backspace to the error, make the correct keystroke, and the mistake will vanish! Insert and delete are simple keystrokes now.

Instead of having to choose between sending out your text with errors intact, or waiting for it to be typed from scratch—you get letter-perfect text quickly. With your new word processor, you can type a text at your fastest rough-draft rate. And forget about transpositions, omissions, and all the other little mistakes that used to slow you down when you typed on a standard electric. With your new word processor you can easily fix errors—a letter, word, line, or paragraph at a time. When you need to make revisions, you can move paragraphs and add text, while rearranging margins, paragraphs or column indents, and line spacing—all before you commit a single character to paper.

And It Has Memory!

After you have completed typing your document, you can ask your word processor to print it out on paper. Simply give it a special command, and—presto!—you'll get your printout exactly as it appeared on the display screen. No surprises. You can also ask it to store the page away. What a convenient filing system! Electronic filing at your fingertips. Now, instead of adding carbon copies to a bulky filing cabinet, you type letters onto your screen, give them names, and tell your word processor to "memorize them!" When you want to use them again, call them back to the screen, and ask the printer to print out as many copies as you need.

Great for Traditional Typing Jobs

In addition to making it easy to type all your letters, memos, and reports faster, with no errors, your word processor handles all the basic typing jobs you do every day. These include index cards, envelopes, multipage reports, multipart forms, and more. Why keep an extra traditional typing station when your new word processor performs all your standard typing tasks?

Handle Administrative Tasks

Think of your new word processor as your administrative assistant, too. It can handle such varied tasks as:

sorting	designing forms
follow-up lists	creating form letters
calendars and message logs	typing index cards
calculations	internal memos

More Miracles!

If your word processor has a multifunction capability—that is, if it is connected to a computer or network—a whole new world of possibilities is opened up:

- Press a key, type in a few words, and display on the screen the inventory level of bolts of cloth in your factory.
- Press another key, and you'll find out the number of dealers in Los Angeles who carry your products and their sales volumes last year.
- Another key allows you to compare the response to an advertising campaign from year to year.
- Use the numbers on the keyboard and figure out your share of the market in Pittsburgh and what would happen to it if you changed the price schedule.
- Retrieve your alphabetized mailing list, and add two more customers and delete one.
- Press another key, and it shows you all the messages you received. You can call them up in order of importance, read them, and type in replies that will go right back to the senders. No paper to shuffle, because it's all done electronically.

. . . And on and on. At this point you may be overwhelmed by the promises and possibilities of your new word processor. All of the features described in this introductory section exist right now. With your first word processor, you can plug into a more sophisticated, integrated electronic office.

Like a new luxury car, you may be tempted to give it a test drive and hit all the buttons. Be cautious. Go slow! Use only the options and special features of your word processor that you need now. As your business expands, your word processor can become part of the electronic office. It is capable of growing and changing. You can plug new devices into it at will; you can switch around to fit the changing needs of your company. As your business expands and your need for more and accurate information becomes crucial, your word processor stands ready to serve you more than you ever imagined. By using this tool with intelligence and skill, your journey through the automated office will be productive and enlightening.

For any new tool or automated procedure to be successful, you must be considerate and aware of other employees who will come into contact with the word processor. Although this section has emphasized the physical hardware of your word processor, we are still talking about "automation," a word that may have frightening connotations for many people in your office. Before you can do anything about implementing your system into your office, you have to overcome the sociological obstacles that exist in your company. It won't be an easy thing to do, but it can be done. And the secret is to proceed along an evolutionary growth path, one step at a time.

This brief overview of features and capabilities is general in its description. A more detailed and step-by-step approach will be presented throughout this book.

Getting the Most Out of Your Word Processor will help you become more aware of what your word processor can do. You are in for many surprises.

Introduction **1**

A woman in Chicago owns three travel agencies. She'd like to send out more advertising flyers but can't find the time to address them.

A doctor who shares a professional office with two other doctors has recently merged operations into a single entity in New York City. Their medical secretary cannot handle the additional paper work for this expansion.

The president of a small but growing solar energy products company in Pennsylvania had to hire two more clerks to take care of order entries and backlog reports.

A Scarsdale housewife has written three cookbooks and has a contract for two additional books. Her portable typewriter at home restricts her in revising and updating the manuscript every time she wishes to change something.

A Seattle auto parts dealer invests hours reordering necessary but low-margin items.

WHO NEEDS A WORD PROCESSOR ANYWAY!

1

Every two weeks, a Florida contractor gives up three evenings with his family to get the payroll out on time.

The VP of Communications of a major Ohio-based retailing operation is periodically troubled by the disappearance of promotional information and news releases.

A college math professor is an author, consultant, and speaker. Every semester he retypes course outlines, exams, and assignment sheets when they need only minor revisions.

The personnel director of a large New England appliance manufacturer is forever chasing down employee information records for production managers. . . .

All these people have an immediate need for a word processing system. What's more, if each did nothing but solve that one problem, the word processor would pay for itself in less than six months.

Before you say, "It's not for me," think of your own operation for a minute. Think of the tons of paper work, the avalanche of forms, and the flood of information you have to handle to keep your business profitable. How much time and money would you save if, simply by pushing a few keys, you could generate a mailing list, scan your inventory, create a pie chart to highlight a statistical report, or check your employee productivity records? You stand to save plenty! It's not magic. It's using a machine to do the drudgery so that you and your people are free to make decisions for a successful business.

It's technology. That technology has made the modern word processor or information processor simple to learn and given it more flexibility and power than ever before. Today's machines have been designed with the user in mind. They eliminate the mystery, complexity, and expense in order to provide the business world with an essentially simple and universally usable tool.

FIGURE 1-1
U.S. Dept. of Labor predicts that by the year 1990 office workers will outnumber the farmers and laborers of the industrial world.

The Move to the Office.

Farmers and Laborers

Office Workers

U.S. Dept. of Labor predicts that by the year 1990 office workers will outnumber the farmers and laborers of the industrialized world.

HOW IT ALL STARTED

Since its humble beginnings, word processing has expanded from fast document processing to manipulation and sharing of data. An entire chapter in *Word Processing* (Prentice-Hall, Inc.) describes the history of word processing in detail. For our purposes, an exhaustive detailed account can be compressed into a short series of events. The need to automate has been building throughout this century, and word processing provided the justification and implementation to do so. Automation is one way of doing jobs more quickly at a reasonable cost, and the word processor became the primary tool to do the job.

EXTERNAL FORCES

We are no longer primarily an industrial society. More Americans are now in information jobs than in manufacturing and agriculture combined. As the economy shifts from goods to services, the percentage of the so-called "information workers" grows at the

3

FIGURE 1-2
Displaywriter. *Courtesy: IBM*

FIGURE 1-3
Courtesy: International Data Corporation

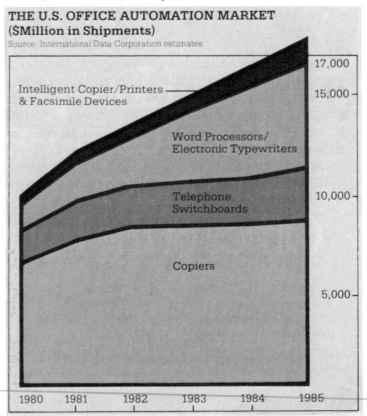

rate of 2 percent each year. By 1990 office workers will outnumber the farmers and laborers of the industrial world. Just look at the glass and steel towers that span the avenues of American cities. Who works there? Information workers.

Today's most pervasive technological trends started with a technological revolution. Before it is over, it will overshadow the industrial revolution in both its scope and its impact on business. Today there is one word processor or electronic typewriter for every five secretary/typists in the U.S. Eventually, Booze, Allen & Hamilton, Inc. estimates that automation will affect 38 million of more than 50 million existing white-collar jobs. This revolution started with the word processor—a magnetic tape typewriter—and with the phrase "word processing." Today, word processing has grown into big business.

By 1985, the market for word and information processors and related peripherals will be $18 billion. This projection can be broken down into the following components: By 1985 there will be in the U.S. 4,000,000 desktop computers, 1,500,000 other computers, and 11,500,000 word processor/computer terminals—many in office applications. The white-collar workforce in 1985 will be 60,000,000 strong. They will work with 27,000,000 office devices—not counting TVs, phones, or hand-held calculators. That's three times as many as were available in 1981.

To begin to understand the boundless promise of your new machine and our new information society, we need to define some terms. *Word processing* is the use of electronic equipment to type, change, and permanently store information for final printing and future use. Word processing is really a process, not just a product; it is an attitude as much as it is an identifiable set of hardware and software. Implicit in this definition are several important ideas, all of which center on the "people, procedures, equipment" concept. Although we will discuss how people and procedures influence and enhance the quality of work life and the value of information, this book focuses on the equipment—our primary tool of productivity.

THE EQUIPMENT The word processor is the information worker's tool. The word processor, like the computer, is the predominant tool of the twentieth century, and possibly for centuries to come. It is an incredible device that allows us to create, store, and revise large amounts of information on a chip one-half the size of a fingernail. Word processors are used by lawyers, writers, and secretaries, in applications that seem limitless.

To understand how the word processor can contribute to improved office productivity, we must accept the fact that the word processor is only a tool—no more and no less. It is the application of this tool, along with the hand that controls the application, that results in productivity.

Many manufacturers of word processing systems are vying for a share of a growing market. The giants include IBM, DEC, Wang, Xerox, and Burroughs. The array of equipment is categorized by the following types: electronic typewriters, blind stand-alone systems, display systems, shared systems, and multifunctional terminals. The blind systems (display-less) that use magnetic tape or cards were once the pioneers of the word processing industry. Today, users of word processors are beginning to subscribe to a "holistic" perspective—where word, data, image, and voice processing are all part of a multifunctional terminal.

FIGURE 1-4
The word processor is only a tool—
no more and no less.

FIGURE 1-5A
Nixdorf 8840/5 is a shared resource word processing system. It consists of a central processor with powerful word processing, software, CRT workstation(s) for permanent document archiving, and a high-speed character printer. *Courtesy: Nixdorf Computer*

FIGURE 1-5B
A shared system

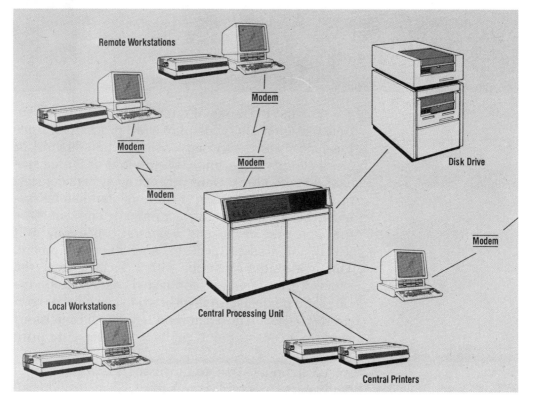

FIGURE 1-6
Philips Micom's 2000/1 standalone word processor was voted
first in its class in a recent Survey of Word Processing Users.
Courtesy: Philips Information Systems

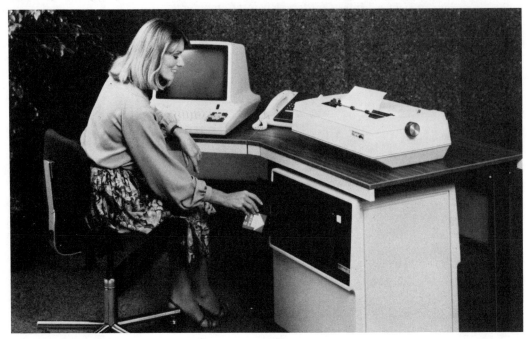

For the purposes of our book, we will concentrate our attention on display word processors, since the majority of systems now being installed in offices are the display type, either stand-alone or *shared system*. A shared logic word processing system consists of workstations, similar to those of stand-alone systems, that are connected electronically and that share the logic and memory of a central processing unit (CPU), the storage medium, and other equipment. The workstations can be either located near the processor or remotely connected, using telephone lines and modems. Any workstation can have its own printer adjacent, or it can send lengthy or repetitious work to a central point, perhaps in a separate print room.

A stand-alone word processor is one that cannot be clustered by a cable connection. We also might call this classification a "pure" or dedicated word processor since its main function is "word processing."

Equipment vendors are offering systems with both data processing and word processing capabilities. The line between data processing and word processing becomes blurred when we try to label the new generation of desktop machines that do multifunction tasks.

There are levels within the business computer categories, and it is important for the user to know and identify his or her "box" to understand the capability. The *business microcomputer* fills the gap in price and performance between personal computers with limited abilities and large minicomputers with great versatility. The former are suitable for individual businesspersons or proprietors working on limited problems; the latter best serve large businesses with many work locations involving large employee populations.

By comparison, personal computers usually sell for $2,000 to $7,000, but even in their most expanded, fully optioned form, they have limited inherent power and applications capabilities.

IS IT A COMPUTER OR WORD PROCESSOR?

FIGURE 1-7
HP-120 personal office computer system from Hewlett-Packard has applications in decision support for management (left), accounting services for small businesses (right). *Courtesy: Hewlett-Packard*

FIGURE 1-8A
Hewlett-Packard HP 125 Computer System. *Courtesy:*
Hewlett-Packard

FIGURE 1-8B
Large-scale computers. *Courtesy: Honeywell*

FIGURE 1-9
A word processing system. *Courtesy: A.B. Dick Co.*

FIGURE 1-10
Wang Professional Computer designed for a new generation of personal computer users. Primarily intended for professionals and managers, the Wang Professional Computer can help virtually every level of office worker throughout an organization make timely, more effective decisions based on the most up-to-date information available. *Courtesy: Wang Laboratories*

Wang describes their devices as a "professional computer designed for the new generation of personal computer users—primarily designed for professionals and managers." (See Figure 1–10.)

At the "high" end, the larger minicomputers and mainframes sell between $50,000 and the million-dollar range. In their stripped configurations they are limited in power. At any size, they require a costly, highly trained staff capable of handling complex computer hardware/software operations. Many of the larger machines also require special-purpose environments that include air conditioning, special flooring, uninterruptible power supplies, and other facilities.

A display word processor consists of three basic parts.

1. A workstation (terminal) with a typewriter keyboard and a screen. The keyboard may be a separate component and may be attached to the console by a coiled cable, so that you can move it to whatever position is most comfortable for you. (See Figure 1–11.)

FIGURE 1-11
The Dictaphone System 6000 word processor has an easy-to-read, tiltable CRT screen, and a separate keyboard for operator ease and comfort. *Courtesy: Dictaphone Corp.*

The CPT 8500 Series word processor. *Courtesy: CPT Corporation*

The display screen, sometimes called a CRT (cathode ray tube), resembles a TV picture tube that displays the information being held in the system. As the operator keyboards text, the characters appear on the screen and the operator is able to watch each operation that is performed while keyboarding.

2. A microprocessor or central processing unit (CPU) with special capabilities to store documents as they are created and later to recall them for revisions. The microprocessor may be a separate box (see Figure 1–12), or it can be built into the chassis of the workstation terminal. (See Figure 1–13.)

FIGURE 1-13
The NBI System 3000 word processor. *Courtesy: NBI Corp.*

FIGURE 1-14
96-character print wheel.
Courtesy: Qume Corp.

FIGURE 1-15
Thimble print elements.
Courtesy: NEC Corp.

3. Offices are a long way from becoming "paperless," and most tasks require hard paper copy output. Thus, *printers* are a necessary part of the word processing system to produce documents at high speeds. Printers have not changed much since the early 1970's when the daisy wheel was introduced by Diablo. The daisy wheel typing unit is a 3-inch diameter disk, with typewriter letters on spokes radiating from the wheel's center. 'See Figure 1–14.) It can print up to 55 characters per second compared to just 15 for IBM's Selectric metal ball, previously the standard in the industry. The daisy wheel is an impact printer. In other words, the characters are printed out by striking an inked ribbon, which leaves a pattern on the paper. Several other impact printers are on the market, and some of them use different print elements, such as the thimble print element. (See Figure 1–16.) The daisy wheel, however, is the element that is used the most in printers and electronic typewriters.

When you consider purchasing a word processing system for the first time, or upgrading your pres-

FIGURE 1-16
The Sprint 9 printer. *Courtesy: Qume Corp.*

ent system, you should decide which type of printer will serve your purpose. Daisy wheel, matrix, and line printing are the three basic technologies used today in most character printing applications. And they vary as much in print quality as they do in technology. Just compare the actual, unretouched close-ups of characters printed by terminals using different printing technologies in Figure 1–17.

Printers, an important facet of the word processing system, are often the component that can cause the most trouble to the user. Although printer technology is still in its infancy, several exciting technological developments bear watching including laser printing and fiber optics.

For users who are not interested in high-speed printing, but who do want letter quality, Smith-Corona offers a low-price letter quality printer that can be connected to most word processors and personal computers. (See Figure 1–18.) For those not interested in letter quality printing, substantial savings can be accomplished by purchasing low-cost line and dot-matrix printers.

Line
Printer

Matrix
Printer

Ink Jet
Printer

Daisy Wheel
Letter Quality
Printer

FIGURE 1-17
Comparison of printer technology

FIGURE 1-18
Smith-Corona TP-1 printer. *Courtesy: SCM Corp.*

FIGURE 1-19
Radio Shack TRS 80 line printer Model V. A high-speed bidirectional, logic-seeking, dot-matrix printer with printing speeds of up to 160 characters per second. *Courtesy: Radio Shack Corp.*

FIGURE 1-20
Radio Shack TRS Line Printer VIII. This is a compact, high-density, dot-matrix impact printer with print speed of 40 to 100 cps. *Courtesy: Radio Shack Corp.*

HOW YOUR WORD PROCESSOR WORKS   As you enter data with your keyboard, the characters, words, numbers, symbols, and (sometimes) graphics are displayed on the screen. Temporarily held in the buffer (a sort of temporary holding bin), the text is

then proofread and errors are corrected. You can delete or add sentences, move paragraphs, or jump from
page to page in a multipage document. Once you are
satisfied that the data are ready to be printed out, or
recorded on the storage or flexible (floppy) disk, you
can give the appropriate command, and the system
will complete the cycle.

Storage media, which are among the supplies and
accessories for your word processor, will be covered
extensively in a later chapter. A brief explanation at
this point will clarify a necessary and important component of the equipment. Storage media, which usually consist of a flexible disk that is sometimes called
a floppy disk, allows the operator to record and store a
collection of documents. A flexible disk is a circular
piece of plastic inside a tough paper cover. (See Figure 1–21.)

THE STORAGE MEDIA

FIGURE 1-21
Anatomy of a floppy disk. *Courtesy: 3M Data Recording Products
Div.*

Saving time and money
. . . the inside story:

Polyvinyl (PVC) jacket protects
against handling damage and
provides crack resistance over
an operating range of 50°-125°F.

Fabric Liner helps keep disk
free of dust and other
contaminants.

Low modulation provides better
signal stability and reduced
peak shift for concise, reliable
performance.

Smooth surface means better
head-to-disk contact for
uniform signal output. 3M
diskettes measure less than 3
microinches.

Increased durability means
long-term reliability under
heavy use.

Low abrasivity extends the life
of read/write heads for longer
performance, reliability, and
lower operating costs.

Stress relief notches on the
bottom edge help prevent
creases and resist damage,
even after repeated handling.

Better
performance is yours,
if you handle with care.

Handle the diskette by the jacket
only — never touch the diskette
recording surface.

Keep the diskette away from
magnetized objects, motors, and
power cables.

Use a fiber-tip pen to write on
diskette labels already applied —
never pencils or ball-point pens.
Do not erase.

Write on label *before* placing it
on the diskette.

Keep the diskette out of direct
sunlight and away from
excessive heat.

Do not use paper clips or rubber
bands on the diskette.

Do not bend or fold the diskette,
or place heavy objects on it.

Insert the diskette by grasping
the upper edge and placing it
carefully into the drive.

Store diskettes on edge in the
specially designed containers.

Some word processors use no external media. They are self-contained in the word processor. That is, they have "internal memory." Electronic typewriters, for example, have internal memory that stores keystrokes on a small silicon chip. A more complete explanation is presented in a later section of this chapter.

Internal memory word processors capture the keystrokes, as well as the format functions (such as tab sets and carrier returns), and special coding instructions (such as deleting an unwanted word or centering a line of copy) for future playback. Electronic typewriters using internal memory have limited storage capacity—usually four to five pages.

FIGURE 1-22
Shugart's SA 600 series of 5¼-inch Winchester disk drive offers storage capacities of 3.33, 6.66, and 10 megabytes. *Courtesy: Shugart Associates*

Another example of a word processor that does not use external media employs the *rigid* or *hard disk* media storage feature. This is a system whereby a rigid disk is built into the disk cabinet and is not intended to be removed by the operator. It has a very large storage capacity. Like most new technology, the rigid disk does not sound like much. Technically, it is called a micro Winchester drive or rigid micro disk drive. Most of these disks use a 5¼-inch metal memory disk. It is both a challenger and a companion to the floppy disk drive system.

The rigid disk drive's primary attraction is its vast storage capacity on its 5¼-inch surface, not coincidentally the size of most floppy disks. It is capable of storing up to 10 million bytes, or characters, of memory—the equivalent of three large novels. Compare this with the 143,000 to 250,000 bytes of memory that a one-sided floppy disk can store. The added storage of the micro Winchester transforms a small word processor or a personal computer from a "mom-and-pop" operation to a substantial business.

BUFFER MEMORY

All computers and word processors use at least some working memory to support such functions as operator input, processing, and output. The working memory may also be called the *buffer memory*, which is an important part of your word processor. Acting as an intermediary between input, magnetic media, and output, it provides the operator with an area in which to edit input and manipulate recorded documents. The information that will be used later is stored inside the equipment until it is transferred to the on-line processor. The material is stored on a working memory chip. A miniature electronic chip, as explained in the previous section, may be smaller than your little finger, yet have the capacity to store up to 64,000 characters. The ability to store in a buffer increases the capacity of the equipment.

Just what is a chip and why is it important for the function of our word processor?

One of the most important components of your word processor is a small but powerful piece of electronics called a silicon chip. It is really a miniature computer known as a microprocessor, and it is housed on a tiny silicon chip. It has the ability to perform millions of calculations or to issue millions of instructions in a

ELECTRONIC CHIPS— THE MIRACLE OF STORAGE AND MEMORY

FIGURE 1-23
16-bit bipolar microprocessor. *Courtesy: Advanced Micro Devices*

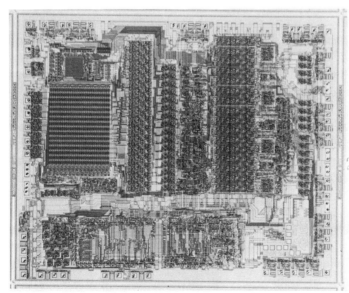

FIGURE 1-24
The Intel 2732 stores 32,768 bits of ultra-violet erasable and electrically programmable read-only memory. *Courtesy: Intel Corp.*

single second. Thousands of tiny electronic functions are imprinted on wafers by photographic and chemical processes. The chips are stacked in modules, which, when connected, allow performance of desired functions. Programs may be stored on special permanent memory chips known as read-only memory (ROM).

PROGRAMS: EXPANDING THE CAPABILITIES OF YOUR WORD PROCESSOR

Programs entered from diskettes are usually called "software." The term *software* refers to a program that controls the operations of word and data processing equipment. The term *hardware* refers to the equipment.

A variety of industry and customer software packages can upgrade your present word processor by simply acquiring the appropriate package for your needs. Such new programs may have math or records processing capabilities, or they may contain dictionaries. The new instructions on diskettes are simply inserted into your equipment to provide new and greater capabilities.

SOFTWARE—THE HEDGE AGAINST OBSOLESCENCE

In the face of ever-changing technology, a word processor owner can become somewhat bewildered by learning that something better, cheaper, with more bells and whistles will be introduced next year, next month, or next week.

My dad bought a black and white television set in 1947. It was a small RCA table-top model that cost $440. A lot of money in those days. We were the first family on the block to own a TV set. For us, it was an exciting and entertaining new technology. Some of our neighbors, however, thought it was a foolish purchase. "TV is not perfected yet. Besides there are not enough programs to make it worthwhile." "It's too costly." "I am going to wait a few more years for the price to drop." These were some of the remarks. My dad probably knew all those things, but his reasoning was—"So what! I want my family to enjoy the TV now, and not to worry about improved versions, more programs, or a drop in price next year, or five years from now." The same reasoning can be applied to your present word processor. Owners know that better, cheaper, and more versatile systems will be introduced, but they should stick with their present system for at least a "payback period."

The best defense against obsolescence is that your word processor is "software programmable." Today most systems are software programmable, which means that a user can add to or upgrade a machine's capabilities through the use of software packages that are stored on the system's diskette or other medium. You simply load a diskette with the correct software program—such as records management, graphics, or finance—into your system. When the program is no longer needed it can be removed and a different program can be entered.

Imagine if systems were not upgradable. It would cost a user or a company a fortune to upgrade their word processing box every time they needed a different application. Amy Wohl, President of Advanced Office Concepts, a Bala Cynwyd, Pennsylvania consulting firm, says, "Users who must be the first to use each new technology aren't running a pioneer office automation site—they're running chaos."

Basic Features and Functions 2

The modern word processor should perform three primary functions:

1. fast document production—especially the production of repetitive documents that can be stored and retrieved;
2. fast and flexible document revision, using the text editing features available in every word processing system; and
3. the printing of finished-quality documents at high speeds.

All of these goals can be accomplished by using the basic features and powerful word processing capabilities inherent in modern word processors.

Probably the most tedious, time-consuming, error-prone task in your office is *keyboarding*: letters, proposals, reports, orders, invoices, and manuals. The flow is endless. That is why, through intelligent use of some of the features of your word processor, you can now find a better way to handle the mass of words that flow through your organization (or your desk) every day, thus making your office operation much more efficient.

Of the many different word processing systems, each product has special features and functions that are placed differently on the keyboard, that operate differently, and that use different coding procedures. Therefore, this chapter will not explain everything you need to know about all word processors. The functions and features in this chapter are aimed at building your overall understanding. The information is general, and, by presenting it to you in a generic way, it will help you to understand what functions you can expect to find in almost any word processor. You should also understand what these functions do, and why they are a part of your word processor. The knowledge you gain from this chapter combined with an understanding of your specific operator's manual will make it easier for you to become productive on a wide range of applications.

Our starting point will be the *keyboard*. This is the component of your word processor that you will be using constantly. Some keyboards are attached to the screen directly, and others are separate components attached to the screen by a coiled cable. All keyboards will have the familiar standard keyboard configurations—commonly referred to as the QWERTY keyboard. Also, some parts of the keyboard may be unfamiliar to you. These special keys may be located at the side of your standard keyboard or on the top row. These special keys may be a different shade or color, and they control the word processing functions.

THE KEYBOARD TOUCH

The "touch" of your keyboard reacts instantly, generating an electronic signal in the form of characters on the screen. A very different sensation from a traditional typewriter, the word processing keyboard responds quickly and quietly, and you will find you are typing (keyboarding) faster on your word processor than on your traditional electric typewriter.

To add to the continuity of rapid keyboarding, most word processors provide an automatic wraparound feature. As you keyboard, you need not worry about hitting the return key to end the typed line. As each line of text is filled, the system automatically moves the *cursor* (lighted symbol on your screen that shows the exact placement within your document) and your typed entries to the next line. All word processing terminal keyboards *do* have a return key to use when you want to indicate a return in a specific place in the text. Your main use for this key is to indicate the end of paragraphs and/or extra lines between paragraphs. With the wraparound feature, keyboarding becomes a high-production, worry-free task.

WORD WRAPAROUND

Most word processors have a set of keys called "cursor control keys" or "directional arrows." The purpose of these keys allows you to move the cursor (the equivalent of a "carriage" on a typewriter and usually represented by a "short arrow") in four directions—north, east, south, and west. (See Figures 2–1 and 2–2.) If you touch one of these keys once, the cursor moves a single space in the direction indicated. If you hold the key down, the cursor moves repeatedly, at full keyboard speed.

CURSOR CONTROL KEYS

FIGURE 2-1

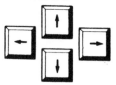

FIGURE 2-2
Cursor (movable in four directions)

EDITING AND REVISION

Keyboarding and editing functions are easy to perform on your screen system, because most systems offer fluid cursor control (as explained above) coupled with horizontal and vertical scrolling. The primary advantage of screen systems over typewriter-oriented systems is the ease and efficiency with which corrections and/or revisions in text can be made. While keyboarding, if you make a mistake, simply backspace and strike over the correct character or characters. You can also use the *delete* function (Delete key). To delete text, you simply move your cursor to the spot in the document you wish deleted, and by a command you can delete a character, word, line, paragraph, or any remainder of text. When the deletion is complete, and the correct command is executed, the material on the screen wraps up to fill in the empty space.

You can combine the delete function with the continue or repeat function, and "gobble" up characters to the right of the cursor location at the rate of about 10 cps (characters per second). You can, of course, also move your cursor on your word processor to strike over or insert material.

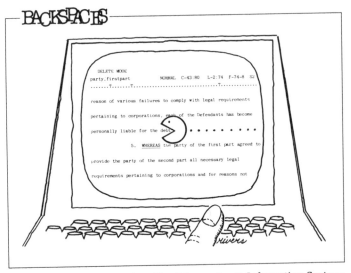

Reproduced with permission: *Word Processing & Information Systems* Geyer-McAllister Publications, Inc., 51 Madison Avenue, New York, NY 10010 (October 1982), p. 56.

To insert text, you place the cursor where you want to begin adding material, and press the Insert key. The remainder of that line and the rest of the text (from the cursor position) drops down, leaving a blank space on the screen. If your insertion takes up more space than furnished, the system will automatically continue to "open" lines to provide room. To get out of the insert mode, you have to depress another key (Insert again, cancel, Execute or Return).

Two other features relating to the editing function that promote operational ease are the "Help" and "Undo" functions. Touching *Help* on the keyboard causes an explanation of application functions to appear on the screen. An *Undo* command enables the operator to cancel the latest input and retrieve earlier versions of work in progress.

SCROLLING

Scrolling text on your word processor allows you to see a different portion of the text than appears on the screen, because the text can be rolled (scrolled) upward or downward. This feature is like turning the pages of a typewritten document. Instead of rolling the paper up or down on a standard typewriter, you can enter commands that enable you to move up and down on your word processor. Scrolling may be useful in proofreading. If you move the cursor up or down one line at a time, the text scrolls one line at a time.

NEXT SCREEN FEATURE

Closely related to scrolling, and also the equivalent of turning the pages of a typewritten document, is the *Next Screen* or *Next Page* function. Just as pages need to be turned during the reading of a document, this function enables you to move the text forward to a new screenload. It occurs on some word processors when the bottom of the screen is reached. A new screen is automatically displayed with the last three lines from the previous screen carried over. To back up to the previous screen, simply touch a special Previous Screen key.

CANCEL FUNCTION

Sometimes you may be in the middle of a revision command or cycle, and you decide to change your mind. Most word processing systems have a "way out" or "change-of-mind" key. It may be called an Escape Key, a Cancel Key, an Undo key (as has been already explained), or even an Oops key. When it is depressed, the system stops what it is doing and puts itself into standard text-entry mode.

TO MOVE A BLOCK OF TEXT

The move function allows you to alter text by rearranging the order of sentences and/or paragraphs to improve meaning and coherency. With a word processing system, it is easy to move sentences, paragraphs, or whole blocks of text within a document. You can do this by first defining the portion to be moved with the appropriate function key.

Once the text is defined[1] you position the cursor at the point where you want this text to be inserted. Finally, you simply depress a function key and the new text is automatically inserted into position. If you change your mind and wish to remove the originally moved text, you can always do so by coding the move sequence again.

FORMAT STORAGE

Format storage includes margins, tab setting, paragraph indentions, and line spacing. Many word processing systems have formats preset; that is, they are already established to provide you with common settings such as:

---

[1]Defined text may be highlighted by a reverse video or "halftone" effect, or they stand out by being extra bright.

- Side margins—set at one inch
- Tab settings—set at five spaces along the horizontal line
- Line spacing—set at single spacing

Format storage settings can be changed, of course, by the operator.

This feature enables you to create and store either one or more phrases or a series of vocabulary words. Phrase storage is also called "glossary" function, and the word processing user can build an electronic library of frequently used terms, so that these entries can be called up and automatically inserted as a document is being created or edited. You can readily see the time saved in using the phrase storage feature. A secretary could store a frequently used closing entry if the same closing was needed for 30 letters a day.

PHRASE STORAGE (GLOSSARY)

Very truly yours,

AJAX PLUMBING CORPORATION

John Reed, Vice President

Instead of 73 keystrokes, only 2 keystrokes would be required—the Glossary key and the special character key assigned for this entry.

For instance, a financial analyst generating correspondence to clients might store such words and phrases as:

- Money Market Fund
- IRA
- Short-term cash needs

- Sincerely,

  John Matuse
  Account Executive
- The current rate of interest is
- You can open an account with as little as
- THE ABC MONEY MARKET ACCOUNT
  3 Westhaven Plaza
  West Los Angeles, CA 94002

An opthamologist might store such words and phrases as:

- retina
- cornea
- iris
- posterior chamber
- anterior chamber
- dilated pupils
- Our records indicate that you are due for your annual eye examination on
  Please call our office for an appointment.

These could be of great use in medical reports, histories, and patient correspondence.

LONGER PARAGRAPHS: MERGING STANDARD PASSAGES

The phrase and glossary feature can be expanded and enlarged to provide easy assembly of documents that include standard passages of information. You can easily maintain an electronic library of standard passages that your office reuses. To assemble a new document using some of these standard passages, just type in the passage numbers or names. Your word processor will assemble them for you in the order you request.

If you need to insert some custom-written material too, simply type it between the standard passage numbers or names. There is no need to worry about matching formats when inserting new entries. Your system automatically adjusts the format of your standard material to that of your final document. You can choose whether to print, display, or store your final assembled document. With this widely useful function, you also can maintain mailing lists. You can even assemble personalized form letters.

You can center titles easily, using an automatic centering feature. Automatic centering allows you to center words or phrases within the horizontal boundaries of your screen (or margins). On some systems, the centering functions are executed before keyboarding; on other systems, the centering functions are executed after keyboarding.

AUTOMATIC CENTERING

This feature permits the user to automatically underscore a word or a group by entering the underscore code. There are two kinds of underscoring:

AUTOMATIC UNDERSCORING

solid underscoring and

broken underscoring, in which only

words are underlined.

You can align decimal points for columnar formats automatically, using a decimal alignment feature. Constant planning and backspacing is eliminated. *Automatic decimal alignment* allows numbers to be entered in tabulated form without the need to align the decimal point position, making all of the decimal points fall in the same vertical position.

AUTOMATIC NUMBER ALIGNMENT

With this feature you can call for automatic hyphenation and not have to worry about the decisions it makes. Such a feature contains a built-in exception dictionary to handle all those words that do not follow logical hyphenation rules. The hyphenation feature automatically supplies a hyphen in a word at the right-hand margin, then waits for you to position the hyphen as desired.

AUTOMATIC HYPHENATION

AUTOMATIC FOOTNOTING

Modern word processors let you footnote without embedding any codes or going back later to construct the footnotes. It works by automatically typing a footnote to the item to which it pertains, so that if the item is moved to another page, the footnote automatically moves with it without further operator intervention.

SEARCH, REPLACE, AND GLOBAL REPLACE

An entire text can be quickly and automatically scanned for a specific word and phrase. The appropriate change will be made every time it appears. This feature permits searching through a document for a repeated occurrence of a group of characters and replacing it with a new group of characters without the need for the operator to search page by page or line by line for each occurrence.

A *global replace* feature is one of the most powerful features of a stand-alone word processor. Not only will it search through a multipage document automatically, it will perform dozens of changes simultaneously. It will locate and replace multiple character strings within running text, or within specific columns of information. For example, to set up a global search/replace specification for implementation within a regular text, you might enter these combinations:

Search Sequence and Replacement Sequence

Apartment	Condominium
BOWLING ALLEY	BOWLING LANES
Older people	Senior citizens
ESSO	EXXON
Typewriting	Keyboarding
Cop	Police Officer
Secretary	Administrative Assistant

The system recognizes the distinction between upper and lower case characters in the search string, and honors them in the replacement string. In the preceding example, the word processor would locate occurrences of BOWLING ALLEY and replace them with BOWLING LANES.

MERGE APPLICATIONS

The merge feature allows the operator to combine stored text, such as a list of names and addresses, with a stored letter. The merge feature is one of the strongest and most frequently used features of any word processor. The applications are unlimited and beautiful customized letters and memos can be created and printed with speed and efficiency.

TYPING BOLD CHARACTERS

Word processing systems can type boldface with varying intensity—from one- to nine-character overstrikes to fifteenth copy in bold such as:

```
1 overstrike

3 overstrikes

5 overstrikes
```

JUSTIFICATION

Justification is the ability of your word processor to produce printout with an even right-hand margin. This may be achieved by interword spacing (leaving extra white space between words), or by intercharacter spacing with proportionally spaced characters that provide output with a more printlike appearance.

On most visual display systems, the text will be displayed on the screen with an uneven right margin during text processing, but during printing, the system justifies the margins by inserting spaces between words. Text with a center instruction, a flush right instruction, or a return will print as displayed.

```
Nonjustified Text                    Justified Text

xxxxxxxxxxxxxxxxxxxxxxxxxxxxxxxxxx    xxxxxxxxxxxxxxxxxxxxxxxxxxxxxxxxx
xxxxxxxxxxxxxxxxxxxxxxxxxxxxxxxx      xxxxxxxxxxxxxxxxxxxxxxxxxxxxxxxxx
xxxxxxxxxxxxxxxxxxxxxxxxxxxxxxxxxx    xxxxxxxxxxxxxxxxxxxxxxxxxxxxxxxxx
xxxxxxxxxxxxxxxxxxxxxxxxxxxxxxxx      xxxxxxxxxxxxxxxxxxxxxxxxxxxxxxxxx
```

SUBSCRIPTS AND SUPERSCRIPTS Some word processors position superscript characters in one-half space increments. Such devices do not actually raise or lower the letters and numbers on the display but use some kind of flag instead. Superscript and subscript commands on more advanced word processing systems, however, have the effect of positioning numbers or lower case characters one-quarter space above or below the characters.

One-Half Space Increment   One-Quarter Space Increment

Footnote^1 Footnote^1

PAGINATION Pagination can be performed in either manual or automatic mode. Basically, pagination allows the system to bring to the screen the amount of material that will fit within the specified page depth. It allows you to position the cursor at a desired breakpoint and then to store the page away. If there is additional copy on

FIGURE 2-4
Automatic pagination

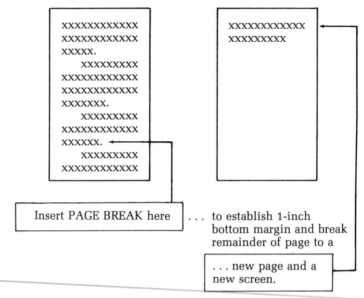

the screen below the cursor location when the page break command is given, the system simply moves that text to the top of the display, appending text from the remainder of the document to again attain the desired page depth.

Let's say you have completed typing a document on the screen, and you realize that your bottom margin is not wide enough to make an attractive page. You can simply position your cursor two or three lines above the last line, and execute the appropriate *Page Break* command. This will immediately give you the correct bottom margin and move the two or three lines to a new page and a new screen.

Automatic Pagination works the same as manual pagination, but does not require operator intervention. The system calls each page of material onto the screen, and "casts it off" at the exact depth specified. If you don't like any of the automatically generated page breaks, you can call the document back from disk and change the breaks manually.

Advanced Software Features **3**

Software is the package that can upgrade your word processor to perform special functions and applications. As described in Chapter One, purchasing software (usually in the form of diskettes), and inserting the program into the word processor, will expand the capability of the equipment. The ability to constantly update your system by adding the latest software keeps your equipment from becoming technologically obsolete. Some of the advanced software features for word processors are:

SOFTWARE— THE KEY TO FLEXIBILITY

1. math package,
2. list processing,
3. records management,
4. forms creation,
5. graphics,
6. glossary,
7. checking of spelling,

8. security, and

9. proportional printing.

Math Package

A good math package can be one of the strongest assets to a word processor user. It allows you to work with columns of figures, which can be added, subtracted, multiplied, and divided, or it can simply verify the accuracy of the column totals.

Other math packages allow users to replace one column or row of figures with another by typing only the new figures. You can also transpose columns or change formats without retyping any numbers.

List Processing

Business organizations create and use a variety of lists, such as a list of their customers' names and addresses or a list of the organization's employees. However, every time there is a change in an em-

FIGURE 3-1
List Processing. *Courtesy: Wang Laboratories*

ployee's or a customer's status, the list has to be retyped. If you have a list processing software feature on
your word processor, this task becomes automatic. A
list processing feature allows you to create and update lists. The processor prints them out according to
any of the categories you desire. For example, if you
have the names, addresses, ages, sex, and Social
Security numbers of your students stored in your
system, you could command the system to give you a
list of only the females that live in a certain city.

A sort feature will automatically sort information in alphabetic or numeric sequence, in ascending
or descending order.

The list processing capability makes updating
lists easier because all of the information does not
have to be retyped, and this, in turn, makes the lists
more valuable to you or your company.

Records Management

With records management capability, you can establish and maintain customized lists electronically.
Records are tailored to your specific needs. Information is retrieved, and results are printed out in a variety of formats, such as letters, lists, or preprinted
forms. This feature gives you the power that was once
reserved for the computer room. Electronic filing expands the capability of records management through
complete storage, retrieval, communication, and de-
struction of records automatically. This will be discussed in detail in Chapter Six.

Closely related to records management is file
management. The file management feature automatically alphabetizes the document directory by title
before displaying it. Some systems provide for a short
description of each document included in the directory to remind you of all the documents written by
any particular author, or those written on any particular date. Other file management system software provide that files are stored on the diskette in a true
random access fashion and are automatically re-

trieved by the system. The operator simply assigns a text name, reference, and page number for identification.

Records management and file management have the added feature of *sorting*. Sort rearranges in alphabetic or numeric order. Records can be arranged, for example, in alphabetic order by last name or in numeric order by ZIP code. The combination of select and sort enables you to put information into a form tailored to your specific needs.

Creating Forms

A forms software package enables you to prepare such items as invoices, purchase requisitions, and other types of forms. Using a forms package, you can create the standard part of the form and update it when necessary. (See Figure 3–2.)

Graphics

Graphics is the ability to present information in the form of bar charts, pie charts, curves, and other visual displays. The adage that a picture is worth a thousand words is demonstrated effectively when horizontal and vertical solid lines can be used to surround text and to draw flow charts, organizational charts, and so on. Not only can some word processors produce graphics, but they also have the ability to edit text within graphics without disturbing the integrity of the vertical lines.

Beyond the basic word processing functions, some systems now offer information retrieval capabilities so advanced and easy to use, you won't have to learn complex data entry routines. To obtain an answer, the user simply asks the system a question—in plain English. For example, Dictaphone Corporation has introduced this feature, Straight Talk℠ natural language information retrieval with its System 6000 word processor (see Figure 3–3), as a

FIGURE 3-2

A typical form. *Courtesy: Nassau Community College*

NASSAU COMMUNITY COLLEGE MEDIA DEPARTMENT, GRAPHICS UNIT, PROJECT TREATMENT GUIDE

(To Be Completed For All Graphics Projects Requests)

Requesting Department _____   Requested By _____

Ext._____ Title of Project _____

Description and Purpose of Service Requested   _____

_____

_____

_____

_____

_____

_____

_____

_____

_____

TYPE OF VISUAL AIDS REQUESTED

☐ 35MM SLIDES/35MM B/W PRINTS   ☐ GRAPHICS FOR TV

☐ OVERHEAD TRANSPARENCIES   ☐ POSTER DESIGN

☐ BROCHURE, PAMPHLETS OR PUBLICATIONS COVER ☐ GRAPHICS FOR FLYERS

☐ GRAPHICS FOR DISPLAYS OR EXHIBITS   ☐ FILM S8 OR 16MM LIVE ACTION

☐ GRAPHICS FOR NEWSLETTER   ☐ FILM S8 OR 16MM ANIMATED

                                        ☐ MISCELLANEOUS

PRIMARY USE

☐ INFORMATION   ☐ COMMUNITY ☐ CAMPUS TOTAL DISTRIBUTION

☐ INSTRUCTION

          (COMPLETED PROJECT WILL BE VIEWED/USED BY #_____STUDENTS)

Date Submitted _____   Date Needed _____

Assigned To _____ Date _____ Completed _____

Approved By _____ Date _____ Received By _____

Production Log-Job Progress	Hours	
Date	In	Out

FIGURE 3-3
The Dictaphone System 6000 word processor uses natural language software to retrieve information. *Courtesy: Dictaphone Corp.*

software option. If personnel records are maintained on your system to facilitate producing personnel-related forms of correspondence, the employee relations manager could type a few simple questions and quickly obtain a plot of employee demographic groupings to satisfy a government information request. This task may have previously required several hours of manual data gathering and interpretation.

Presenting sales or financial data, or showing inventory shortages in graphic form, would help to clarify business situations. The benefits of presenting information in the form of graphics are innumerable. The avalanche of incomprehensible computer printouts, the lengthy reports, and the deskful of numeric data all seem to fall into place. It is much more appealing when you are able to communicate your ideas in the form of attractive and easy-to-understand pie charts, line drawings, and bar graphs. The meaning is grasped in an instant. Additional uses of graphic applications are presented in Chapter Four.

A summary of the advantages of using graphics generated by word processing and other computer terminals[1] follows:

[1]Potts, Jackie, "Computer Graphics Systems for Business," *Today's Office* (February, 1982).

1. The ability to produce more effective communications by increasing the impact of reports, thereby improving the reader's retention.

2. The chance to make decisions based on relationships and comparisons, which are clearly and concisely shown.

3. The capability to prepare presentations that are professional and attractive with full-color graphics.

4. The ability to highlight significant information and trends.

FIGURE 3-4
Sample document with misspelled words, page number, and line number printed out. *Courtesy: Greenman-Woodard Co.*

GREENMAN-WOODARD CO.
COMMUNICATION PRODUCTS

The Greenman-Woodard SPELLWRITER enables the user to check a document for spelling errors at a rate of 3,000 words per minute or approximately one page every six seconds.

1. First load the supplied dictinary disk into the word processor unit, and communicate to the SPELLWRITER. A front panel light indicates the dictionary is in the loading mode. The specialized vocabulary dictionary is loaded in the same manner.

2. The SPELLWRITER is now ready for copy verificatinn. To verify any copy, communicate the document to the SPELLWRITER. A front panel light indicates that the document is in verification mode.

3. Misspelled words are automatically listed and identified by page and line number on SPELLWRITER's print-out.

4. The user can easily make corrections on the original document.

Words not in the standard dictionary may be typed into the special vocabulary dictionary which when communicated becomes part ot SPELLWRITER's vocabulary.

The price of SPELLWRITER is $2995, which includes the printer shown. A 90 day warranty on parts and labor is provided. SPELLWRITER operates at all the standard communication speeds: 110, 134.5, 300, 600, 1200, 2400, 4800, and 9600 baud.

Thank you for visiting our exhibit at Syntopican X. Now you can type without feer!

```
                        SPELLWRITER

                    WORD        PG LI

                    DICTINARY    1  5
                    VERIFICATINN 1 11
                    OT           1 22
                    FEER         1 31

                        TOTALS
                    WORDS      186
                    PAGES        1
                    MISSPELLED   4
```

200 EAST ONTARIO STREET
CHICAGO, ILLINOIS 60611

312-266-2996

Glossary
(Phrase Library or Paragraph Assembly)

Do you have a lot of stock terms, phrases, or paragraphs that are used repeatedly in your typed material? Do you want to use the same term or block of text repeatedly in the same document? The glossary function enables the user to store frequently used terms or phrases and display them on command on the screen in any position within the document. Terms and phrases may be used over and over again to create wills, contracts, proposals, specifications, or letters. The documents containing standard paragraphs may be of any length, and they may contain any number of paragraphs up to the capacity of the disk.

Spelling Checking Program

This feature speeds the proofreading process by checking the spelling of selected words at the touch of a button. It's fast. Word processors with this software system can check each word in a multipage document against a selected 50,000- to 100,000-word dictionary in seconds per page. Some systems can check the spelling of more than 150,000 words in each of many foreign languages. You can even add your special jargon words or proper nouns to the dictionary.

Spelling checking programs can be purchased as separate packages under several brand names. *SpellStar Dictionary Software Program,* for instance, is part of the CP/M operating system (discussed later in this chapter). *SpellStar* consists of a 20,000-word dictionary. This software program allows additional words to be placed in the dictionary in order to customize its use for a specialized vocabulary. Words that do not appear in the dictionary are marked so the user can determine whether the spelling is correct.

The *Spellwriter* is a separate unit that interfaces with your word processing system. It will electronically verify the spelling of 60,000 standard words plus 20,000 additional specialized vocabulary words at 3,000 words per minute.

FIGURE 3-5
Simply by depressing the key marked "SPELL" on this Compucorp word processor, typists are able to verify and correct instantly the spelling of up to a million English and foreign language words. *Courtesy: Compucorp Corp.*

Finished documents are communicated to the *Spellwriter* unit, and misspelled words are listed and identified by page and line number on a printout for an easy, one-time correction of original text.

Security System

Will more than one individual use the same floppy or hard disk to store typing? Ever worry about someone walking off with the wrong disk and reading the confidential material on it? Security systems on word processors allow each user an individual password which causes typed material to be "scrambled" so that no one else can view or change it no matter how much they know about the system. Password protection restricts access to certain files by assigning passwords only to the personnel allowed to use the files.

Proportional Printing

Proportional printing software produces typed pages that are neat and professional looking every time. Proportional printing varies both the character size and spacing of each character based on the width of the letter. Now, all your work can have a distinctive, professional look. Compare the differences yourself in the appearance between proportional printing and nonproportional printing in Figure 3–6.

FIGURE 3-6
Proportional and nonproportional spacing. *Courtesy: Lanier*

Proportional **Read me first!**

Nonproportional **Read me first!**

SOFTWARE FOR DESKTOP COMPUTERS

Many word processors have a variety of software built into the system. It is comparable to purchasing an automobile and listing the standard features. In other systems, however, the advanced software is optional. This is especially true for the small desktop computers.

Microcomputers and hybrid multifunction terminals have created a growth market for an increasing number of organizations and professionals. What started out as a hobby market in microcomputer kits in the mid-1970s, has grown to a $2.6 billion business that is still on a fast growth track. Oddly enough, these computers are the first data or word processing devices to be embraced by upper-level white-collar workers. As Steven Jobs, chairman of Apple Computer says in one of his full-page advertisements, "The Challenge of our industry is not only to help people learn about the computer, BUT to make it so easy to use that by the end of this decade it will be as common (a personal tool) as the bicycle." Meeting that challenge will take plenty of software. Consequently, many applications programs have become available. A computer or word processor without software is about as useful as a car without a driver.

The CP/M Software Program

Two of the most important types of software are operating systems and applications packages. It takes smart operating system software to organize the power of a word processor or computer, and it takes sharp applications software to apply that power to a specific task. The operating system is the heart and soul of the computer, and the biggest name in microcomputer operating systems is CP/M.

CP/M stands for "Control Program for Microprocessors" and is a set of instructions which controls the operation of the microcomputer. CP/M was developed by Digital Research Corporation. With a million systems in place in the United States and a bustling market in third-party software, CP/M has helped make small desktop computers a potent force in the office automation market.

There are many word processors and microcomputers that are compatible with CP/M. Digital Research, the developer of the CP/M has a special version adopted to run on the IBM Displaywriter. (See Figure 3–8.) Many other traditional word processing companies, such as CPT, Wang, and Lanier are designing their word processors for use with CP/M.

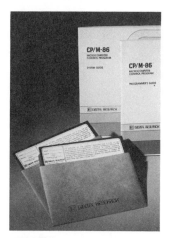

FIGURE 3-7
CP/M-86 software package designed for the IBM Displaywriter. *Courtesy: Digital Research*

FIGURE 3-8
With CP/M, the Wangwriter is a widely accepted operating system for microcomputers, capable of accessing a variety of off-the-shelf software. *Courtesy: Wang Laboratories*

Other business software for word processors—including accounts receivable, general ledger, and inventory management—is available from such independent vendors as Peachtree Software and Lifeboat Associates. In addition, SuperCalc² Electronic Worksheet software is available from another independent software vendor, the Sorcim Corporation, for financial planning and modeling.

WordStar Word Processing Software Package

Part of the CP/M Operating System is the WordStar, a complete word processing software program and the most popular package available. The WordStar package performs all the basic features which stand-alone word processors perform. In addition, WordStar will perform many tasks which stand-alone word processors cannot perform. For example, WordStar can make corrections to existing data processing programs. WordStar can also be used to build data files and to write data processing programs that will use those data files. Other programs that are available to the user of CP/M-based word processing or microcomputer systems are products like Electric Blackboard and The Final Word (two other word processing programs with special features and strengths). The Word is another off-the-shelf software spelling checking program. Grammatik proofreads documents for common grammar and usage errors, and the Random House On-Line Thesaurus is still another choice in a very large selection of programs that perform word processing functions.

An excellent feature for the first-time word processor user is the video screen display of the finished document just as it will be printed. The user can draft a document, make the needed revisions, and see what the final paper copy will look like.

²SuperCalc is a trademark of the Sorcim Corporation.

Combination Software Packages

Some software vendors offer complete software features in a single package. One disk loads several applications at one time. With these packages, there is no need to change disks. A combination software disk may contain specific software applications, such as word processing, math, sorts and others, which can be entered into the internal memory of the system whenever the typist wants to switch applications.

As you can see from our discussion in this chapter, word processing systems can offer the user a lot of power and performance in one box. Some of the software options, like the global replace and the math package, may not be required by all users. The fact is that such well thought-out capabilities are there if and when needed. To the credit of computer scientists and engineers, other interesting programs will be developed to meet your future needs and applications.

SUMMARY

General Applications 4

A. Basic Word Processing Applications

The most frequently used application is correspondence. Correspondence jobs involve the initial capture, correction, revision, and final printing for letters and memos. Word processors are particularly well suited for letters and memos. Even one-page (one-time) letters become effortless. The ability to keyboard, proofread, and make fast corrections and revisions makes the modern word processor an attractive tool for the secretary.

Reports fall into the category of any document other than a letter. Usually, this term refers to a multipage document that has the following features:

REPORTS

1. double-spaced

2. equally balanced margins (top, bottom and side)
3. centered main headings in all capitals
4. flush side headings in consistent style

Included in this kind of application are reports, proposals, contracts, specifications, newsletters and copy for articles and books. Specific applications by industry where word processing has proved particularly effective in generating reports and multipage documents are

- proposals in aerospace and consulting firms
- financial reports in commercial and government organizations
- specifications in engineering firms
- handbooks, instructions, policies for educational and military organizations
- procedure manuals in all organizations
- contracts, wills, pleadings in law firms

Report applications can be processed easily on word processors. The main difference between long and short documents lies in special file management requirements you may encounter. You may find yourself working on documents with texts too long to fit into individual files or even onto single diskettes. It will be up to you to monitor the status of such texts, and to be sure that nothing is lost because of overloading the working memory or the files.

Planning for bottom margin and continuity of pages are automatic features on most word processors. As you keyboard on the screen, the system signals you through prompts or a status line, and it will automatically move to the next page and/or screen. Through automatic headers and footers, it allows you to keyboard a multipage document without worrying about planning for bottom margins and fitting text onto each page. It does so automatically. Entire blocks of text, paragraphs, lines and words can be deleted, inserted, and moved around. The entire manuscript can be rearranged with a press of a button.

Periodic changes can be effected easily. Even after the document has been recorded on your disk, revisions can be made quite easily by simple commands without having to rekeyboard the entire document. In updating quarterly or yearly reports, for instance, columns of numbers can be moved—which saves re-entering each column of figures that needs to be retained for the new report.

FORM LETTERS AND MASS MAILINGS

Probably the most useful application feature of word processing is the ability to create repetitive, individual letters or other documents from file elements stored within the system. Sometimes called power typing, merge, or list processing, it allows text from two documents to be combined during printout. The most common example of this feature is the merging of a standard letter (primary document) with a list of names and addresses (variables or secondary document).

The first step in a merge operation is to create the primary document. This contains everything that is common to every letter, and it contains the merge codes for variable information. The primary document is created once and may be stored on a disk. Figure 4–1 illustrates a sample of a primary document.

The next step is to create a variable document. This contains the information that will replace the merge codes in the letter with specifics for each copy of the standard letter. A sample variable document is as follows:

Mrs. Mary Baumann
One Center Street
Huntington Station, NY 11746 (M)
Mrs. Baumann (M)
Hunting Station (M)

Mrs. Patricia Reilly
6800 Jericho Turnpike
Syosset, NY 11791 (M)
Mrs. Reilly (M)
Syosset (M)

Merging the two documents together is an output procedure. They are actually merged at the printer.

FIGURE 4-1
Primary document

June 18, 19--

(Variable)

Dear (Variable):

We are having an ORIENTAL RUG SALE you cannot afford
to miss: From Thursday, July 1, to Saturday, July 3.
We are inviting you, our valued customer, to a PRIVATE
SHOWING AND SALE.

You will not see a larger selection of fine oriental rugs
on Long Island.

The sale, which is at the (Variable) store only, will be
advertised to the general public on Sunday, July 4, so
be sure to hurry in before then for this extraordinary
event.

Shaw's charge, MasterCard, Visa, and American Express
are welcome. Quality oriental rugs from all over the
world have been a tradition at F. & R. Shaw, where
furniture is an investment.

Sincerely yours,

Ann Roberts
Store Manager

xx

FIGURE 4-2
Mrs. Baumann's individualized letter

```
                        June 18, 19--


Mrs. Mary Baumann
One Center Street
Huntington Station, NY 11746

Dear Mrs. Baumann:

We are having an ORIENTAL RUG SALE you cannot afford
to miss:  From Thursday, July 1, to Saturday, July 3.
We are inviting you, our valued customer, to a PRIVATE
SHOWING AND SALE.

You will not see a larger selection of fine oriental rugs
on Long Island.

The sale, which is at the Syosset store only, will be
advertised to the general public on Sunday, July 4, so
be sure to hurry in before then for this extraordinary
event.

Shaw's charge, MasterCard, Visa, and American Express
are welcome.  Quality oriental rugs from all over the
world have been a tradition at F. & R. Shaw, where furni-
ture is an investment.

                        Sincerely yours,


                        Ann Roberts
                        Store Manager

xx
```

The system prints an individualized copy of the standard letter for each set of variables as shown in Figures 4–2 and 4–3.

FIGURE 4-3
Mrs. Reilly's individualized letter

```
                        June 18, 19--


Mrs. Patricia Reilly
6800 Jericho Turnpike
Syosset, NY 11791

Dear Mrs. Reilly:

We are having an ORIENTAL RUG SALE you cannot afford
to miss:  From Thursday, July 1, to Saturday, July 3.
We are inviting you, our valued customer, to a PRIVATE
SHOWING AND SALE.

You will not see a larger selection of fine oriental rugs
on Long Island.

The sale, which is at the Syosset store only, will be
advertised to the general public on Sunday, July 4, so
be sure to hurry in before then for this extraordinary
event.

Shaw's charge, MasterCard, Visa, and American Express
are welcome.  Quality oriental rugs from all over the
world have been a tradition at F. & R. Shaw, where furni-
ture is an investment.

                        Sincerely yours,


                        Ann Roberts
                        Store Manager

xx
```

STANDARD PARAGRAPHS Sometimes called phrase storage or glossary function, this feature, explained in Chapter Two, allows the word processor user to build an electronic library of frequently used terms and phrases. Merging these phrases into letters and other documents is a valuable time-saver. Examples of applications follow:

Standard Paragraphs Stored in the Office of the County Comptroller—Health Insurance Unit

1. Items submitted by you in filing for a Medical Claim under the County Health Insurance Program, are being returned for the following:

2. Please answer questions 1 to 10 and sign blue form PS-425 and complete white worksheet PS4-55 as best you can.

3. Cancelled checks, cash register receipts, or photostats of bills are not acceptable as evidence of expenses. Send original bill.

4. A doctor's note is required for registered nursing service, prosthetic appliances, wheelchairs, braces, etc.

5. Routine eye examinations and eye glasses are not covered.

6. Charges for nonprescription drugs are not covered.

7. Consult, if you can, your immediate Personnel Office for help in completing your claim. Involved questions will be answered by the Health Insurance Office.

8.   Sincerely,

                              Harold Beckstein
                              County Comptroller

A custom letter can easily be created by combining the stored segments into a single letter to a specific customer. For instance, I could combine paragraphs 1, 3, 7, and 8 to send the letter shown in Figure 4–4.

FIGURE 4-4
Comptroller letter

June 26, 19--

Mrs. Pauline Treemont
379 Airlake Parkway
Lakeville, MN 55044

Dear Mrs. Treemont:

Items submitted by you in filing for a Medical
Claim under the County Health Insurance Program,
are being returned for the following:

Cancelled checks, cash register receipts, or
photostats of bills are not acceptable as evidence
of expenses. Send original bill.

Consult, if you can, your immediate Personnel
Office for help in completing your claim. Involved
questions will be answered by the Health Insurance
Office.

Sincerely,

Harold Beckstein
County Comptroller

LISTS (LIST PROCESSING) List applications are ideal for business organizations and individual users to process information that can be structured in the form of:

- name and address lists,
- inventory lists,
- membership lists,
- personnel file lists, and
- customer enquiry files.

List processing is closely related to merge and glossary functions. To define the criteria of lists, as opposed to textual documents, consider the following distinctions of lists:

1. The information is repetitive.
2. The information is structured.
3. The information is the source for a variety of final output styles.

For example, a list containing names, addresses, and other pertinent information of Canadian members of the International Information/Word Processing Association (IWP) can be used to prepare:

1. personalized letters in English or French for selected members,
2. notices of chapter meetings or special committee meetings,
3. lists of members for dues solicitation, or
4. labels for use in mailing items to the members.

Creating lists provides marvelous opportunities to update and change as members are added, deleted, or move. For example, if you have the names, titles, and affiliations of members of the press, you can update your list as changes occur.

Name	Title	Affiliation
1. Dykeman, John B.	Executive Editor	Modern Office Procedures
2. Beninato, Philip	Advertising Rep.	The New York Times
3. Eifler, Thomas	Publicity Manager	Wang Laboratories
4. Gayman, Arden	Editor	Office Equipment & Methods
5. Kleinschrod, Walter	Editor	Office Administration & Automation
6. Seybold, Patricia	Editor-in-Chief	Seybold Report on Office Systems
7. Lindsey, Clifford	Vice President	Dataquest
8. Wohl, Amy	President	Advanced Office Concepts
9. Tunison, Eileen	Editor	Today's Office
10. Kirk, John	Editor	Inside Word Processing

SORT CAPABILITY

The sort feature of a word processor has the capability to sort either alphabetically or numerically. For instance, if you wished to sort the list above alphabetically, by last name, your word processor could rearrange the list automatically as follows:

1. Beninato, Philip
2. Dykeman, John
3. Eifler, Thomas
4. Gayman, Arden
5. Kirk, John
6. Kleinschrod, Walter
7. Lindsey, Clifford
8. Seybold, Patricia
9. Tunison, Eileen
10. Wohl, Amy

If, for instance, a new name—Andrew Pollack of The New York Times, were to be added to the list, the system would automatically insert his name in alphabetical order.

FORMS APPLICATIONS

Business forms can be prepared on your word processor. The master form is created and saved as an ordinary word processing document. Figure 4–5 shows a form created on a word processor.

FIGURE 4-5
Courtesy: Nassau Community College

NASSAU COMMUNITY COLLEGE

Request For College Equipment To Be Taken Off Campus

From: (Type or Print) _____ Date _____

The use of College equipment is limited to the College campus. However, there may be occasions when some equipment (when available) must be used off campus. In that event, this form must be completed in its entirety and forwarded to the Procurement Office, Inventory Control Section, prior to the equipment leaving the College campus. Notify the Inventory Control Section when the equipment is returned to the College.

Nomenclature _____ Decal Number _____

Signature of Borrower _____ Department _____

Length of Loan _____ From: _____ To: _____

Purpose of Loan _____

Required Approvals:

Director or
Department Chairperson Signature _____

Dean or Vice-President Signature _____

Instructions For Use Of This Form:

Requestor must complete this form. Obtain approval signatures from the department Head, (Director or Chairperson), and Dean, or Vice-President, then forward the white copy to the Inventory Control Section. The pink copy is sent to the department Head. The canary copy is retained by the requestor.

Note:

The borrower is liable for the cost of repair or replacement if the equipment is damaged, lost, or stolen.

P&S 22,

SCIENTIFIC TYPING AND MULTILEVEL FORMULAS

Special coding and printwheels allow for scientific typing and multilevel formula applications (Figure 4–6).

FIGURE 4-6
Scientific typing

THE COST OF CAPITAL

Here D_1 is the next dividend, P_o is the current price per share, and g is the expected growth rate. According to assumption 4 above, the percentage of earnings retained, or the retention rate (b), is zero; since g = br, where r is the rate of return on equity, g = br = 0 X r = 0; in other words, the growth rate is zero. This is consistent with assumption 6 above. Note also that $D_1 = (1 - b)(E_1)$, and with b = 0, $D_1 = (1)(E_1) = E_1$. Thus,

$$K_s = \frac{D_1}{P_o} + g = \frac{E_1}{P_o} + 0 = \frac{E_1}{P_o}$$

This equation is on a per share basis; multiplying both the numerator and denominator by the number of shares outstanding (N), we obtain:

$$k_s = \frac{E_1(N)}{P_o(N)} = \frac{EBIT - I}{S} = \frac{\text{Net income available to stockholders}}{\text{Total market value of stock}}$$

Thus, k_s may be defined on either a per share or a total basis.

MATHEMATICAL APPLICATIONS

Mathematical applications combine the features of electronic calculators with those of word processing. Applications ranging from the calculations of percentages, chain discounts, merchandise markup, to banking, payroll, and a variety of financial statements.

Figure 4–7 illustrates a financial application using the math feature of a word processor. Percentages and totals are easily calculated for this Statement of Revenue and Expense.

FIGURE 4-7

STATEMENT OF REVENUE AND EXPENSES

CONFERENCES

198 /198 Fiscal Year
Registration Fee of $150 (Members)

	Margin	
Conference Revenue (Exhibits & Registration)	100%	652,651
Less Conference Expense	54%	353,945
Excess of Revenue Over Expenses	46%	298,706

Projected 198 /198 Fiscal Year
Two Different Fee Levels

	Margin	$150	Margin	$200
Conference Revenue (Exhibits & Registration)	100%	549,695	100%	895,250
Less Conference Expense	88%	485,847	54%	485,847
Excess of Revenues Over Expenses	12%	63,848	46%	409,403

B. Advanced Applications

Some graphics are standard on word processors **GRAPHICS**
if the user merely wants to create straight lines—
vertical, horizontal, and/or diagonal. These are useful
for simple tables, for organization charts (see Figure
4–8), or for systems configurations (see Figure 4–9).

FIGURE 4-8

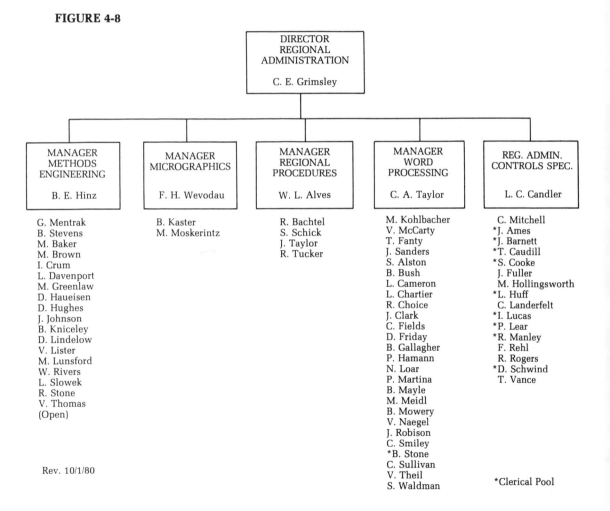

Rev. 10/1/80

FIGURE 4-9
Configuration alternative

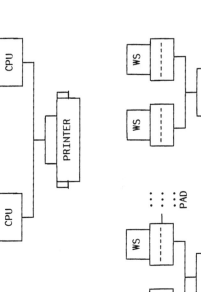
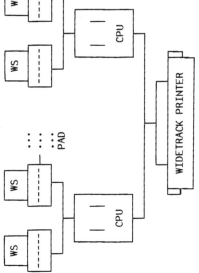
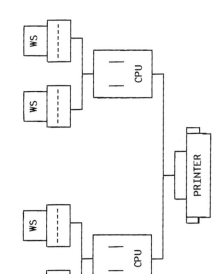
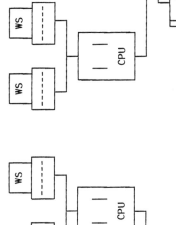
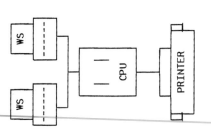

CONFIGURATION ALTERNATIVE

FIGURE 4-10
M-20 personal computer. *Courtesy: Olivetti*

Sophisticated graphics can be offered as a standard feature of some personal computers. Figure 4–10 is a photo of the M-20 Personal Computer from Olivetti. An extremely powerful window command allows the video display to be split into as many as 16 independently controlled "windows," each with full graphic and alphanumeric features.

The availability of graphics on small computers and software packages for discrete word processors provides an easily understood, dramatic, visual presentation of information or of complex interrelationships in a variety of formats.

How graphics can be used effectively is illustrated in the comparison of the memo to Jeffrey Allen from Sam Jablow. How that same information looks in graphic form is shown in Figure 4–11.

FIGURE 4-11A
A textual report compared to a report in graphic form

January 21, 19--

To: Jeffrey Allen

Fr: Sam Jablow

Subject: Comparative Absentee Rate - 3rd Quarter
         19-1 and 3rd Quarter 19-2

As requested during our telephone conversation on January 5th, subject information,
taken from my records, is noted below:

Third Quarter 1982

The July absentee rate was 5.8% for Production Personnel and 6.7% for Office staff.
In August, the Production people developed
a rate of 6.3%, while Office staff dropped
to 5.7%. September's rate was quite high,
probably due to the Jewish holidays. Production was at 8.7%, while Office people
reported 8.9%.

Third Quarter 1983

The July absentee rate was quite low (4.4%)
for the Production Personnel. Office staff
developed a 5.8% rate. The low rate for
Production remained through August with a
4.5% figure. Office personnel recorded
6.0%. Again, due to the Jewish holidays,
September was bit higher. Production reported 6.0%, while Office showed 7.1%.

Further questions? Please call me on extension 533.

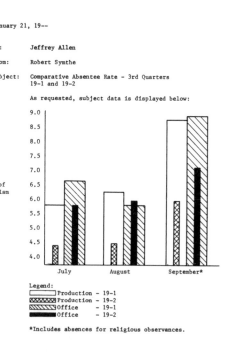

January 21, 19--

To: Jeffrey Allen

From: Robert Symthe

Subject: Comparative Absentee Rate - 3rd Quarters
         19-1 and 19-2

As requested, subject data is displayed below:

% of
absenteeism

Legend:
Production - 19-1
Production - 19-2
Office   - 19-1
Office   - 19-2

*Includes absences for religious observances.

Industry and Personal Applications 5

Word and information processing applications have found their way into every conceivable business from the multipurpose corporation to the small business professional. To survive in this information-intensive society, you as an information worker, manager, or professional, must be concerned with providing the best means to move information and data. Speed, accuracy, and productivity are the obvious goals, and the word processor is the tool that best achieves these goals.

Chapter Four discussed some of the general applications such as correspondence, reports, business forms, and graphics. We will now look into specific businesses, professions, and personal activities to see how word processing (and word processors) can be used to aid information workers in generating their documents with speed and accuracy. The majority of applications involve words, and the manipulation of those words is the pivotal focus of office automation. The primary tool for this is the word processor.

Word processors are becoming easier to use. With varying degrees of success, every vendor is striving mightily to make its machine effortless for the software user. Complex coding and intricate keyboards are now giving way to streamlined and easy-to-use systems. "Help" and "Undo" keys, screen prompts, and programmed learning aids are devices vendors are using to aid managers and first-time users. Built-in dictionaries with the ability to check spelling are a boon to writers and authors.

INDUSTRY APPLICATIONS

Banks

Word processing has revolutionized the banking industry in applications ranging from customer correspondence to lengthy manuals. The primary function of banks is the transfer and storage of money, and every monetary transaction must be supported by documentation and correspondence. Information to customers and officers must be constantly updated and available.

Applications

Most of the typing projects in a bank's office are correspondence. Typical applications are one-page letters to alert customers to a variety of services and to periodic events (monthly account status, quarterly dividends, and new savings plans). Many of these are repetitive documents that involve the handling of money. These documents can be keyboarded and recorded on magnetic disks. When a document is to be sent to a customer, the operator merely recalls the document and inserts the variable information that pertains to the individual (name and address or dollar amount, for example). An example of banking correspondence that is repetitive and convenient for merge applications is shown in Figure 5–1. The following is a list of other bank applications using merge applications:

FIGURE 5-1
Banking correspondence

```
Date: _____

                          Re: _____
                              _____
                              _____

Dear _____:

Kindly be advised that we inadvertantly returned a check
in the amount of $_____ payable to you against the
above account.  Please accept this letter as notifica-
tion that at the time the check was presented for payment,
there funds available, and the check was returned due
to a clerical error.

The subject has been with us for many years and has
always conducted their account in a most satisfactory
manner.

We regret the inconvenience caused you and our depositor.

                          Very truly yours,




                          Julian Bergoffen
                          Bank Manager
```

- Trust Agreement
- Estate Planning
- Overdraft Letter
- Commitment of Loan
- Loan Application
- Payment of Loan Letter
- Collection Letter
- Thank You Letter

- Request for Financial Statement
- Incomplete Application
- Advise New Services
- Welcome New Customers
- Solicit New Business
- Commitment of Mortgage
- Notify of Problem Area in Account
- Request Further Information

In addition to the preceding list, other bank applications include statistical typing, and a variety of financial statements.

Banking Application Trends

Large multicity banks have many offices remote from the central branch. These branches must transport documents and other information back and forth on a daily basis. Because immediacy is important in banking transactions, electronic fund transfer systems and other advanced electronic telecommunications networks for storage and transmission of transaction and summary information have been implemented. These communications systems are a natural adjunct to word processing, and some large banks have begun to integrate their correspondence and management information functions into a total communication system. Forecast modeling and economic projections (including graphics) are a part of these systems. These qualities make them very attractive to officers who need to keep a daily close watch on the fluctuations of the economy.

FIGURE 5-2
Automation in banking. *Courtesy: Honeywell*

Legal Applications

The legal profession recognized the power and versatility of word processing when it was first introduced. Using first-generation word processors, they were able to generate error-free documents in the intricate and precise language of the legal profession. Word processors used in legal applications make the many revisions and move through the many draft cycles that are required. Each draft circulates back to the originating attorney until the document is finally complete and correct. Word processors, through their recording and playback capabilities, allow authors to make extensive revisions. Programs that check the spelling of legal terms are useful to proofread documents. Many systems are equipped with automatic revision-making capability, to facilitate the process of proofreading.

Law firms that engage in heavy litigation practice generate a number of repetitive documents. Paragraphs can be stored and inserted into a variety of standard form contracts. Entire files (libraries of stored phrases and legal terminology) can be categorized and filed. Indexes can then be developed to

FIGURE 5-3
Automation in a legal office. *Courtesy: Data General Corp.*

categorize stored blocks of texts by topic and subject for future cross-referencing. Electronic filing of client documents can be used with advantage as a means for quick storage and retrieval.

Since legal documents can go through many rounds of drafts, high-speed line printers or dot-matrix printers are suitable. When the document is ready for final printout, a lower speed, letter-quality printer is used.

Another legal application of the word processor has come about with legal information banks, such as Lexis, Juris, and Westlaw which are available to attorneys. Subscribers to these services can now search and locate citations and histories on every case from a lower court decision to a U.S. Supreme Court mandate. For more information about Legal Information Banks, contact:

> LEXIS
> A Service of MEAD DATA Central
> 200 Park Avenue
> New York, NY 10017
> (212) 883-8560

Health Services

The care and treatment of patient illnesses provide numerous applications for word processing. The unique nature of medical documentation requires different word processing procedures in hospitals than in other paper-intensive industries. In a hospital environment, the primary source of information revolves around the medical records office and the administrative office.

A large part of a hospital's budget is utilized for word/information processing. From the moment a patient enters a hospital, the paperwork cycle begins. Each medical department within the hospital—Neurology, Psychiatry, Ob/Gyn, and so forth—operates with a certain amount of autonomy, but each depends on an administrative staff for support operations.

A record must be kept of every test administered, every pill taken, every visit by the physician, every vital sign read. The role of the physician goes beyond the examination and treatment of the patient into recording the treatment and processing the information. Modern hospitals use strategically placed computer terminals and word processors to speed paperwork.

Examples of Medical Documents

The majority of documents processed in a hospital involve physician's reports regarding patient admission, treatment, examination, and discharge. Doctors usually dictate at least a medical history, notes on examination, and a discharge summary for each patient. These records are particularly significant as protection against possible malpractice claims. Because these documents are legally binding, their accuracy is extremely important.

Other types of medical documents prepared in the hospital are administrative matters dealing with personal records of staff and physicians, public relations correspondence, and interoffice memorandums. As information grows in a hospital environment, the word processor becomes an increasingly important office tool to standardize and store phrases and medical terminology. This process involves more than simply recording a library of paragraphs. It involves constantly keeping abreast with the latest medical technology and terminology. A method to speed up the report process in patient forms involves storing an examination report for each medical specialty, with all the primary headings recorded as "normal" condition. The attending physician would then simply dictate any sections of the report that corresponded with an "abnormal" patient condition, and the rest of the document would be filled in by the stored text.

Word processing is also finding its way into the private office of the doctor. It alleviates the doctor's

great paperwork burden of endless government and
insurance forms. The doctor, in the daily tasks of
office examination, must also record accurate and
up-to-date patient information. The word processor,
combined with other multifunctional computerized
capabilities, allows the doctor to process billing, store
patient records, process insurance documents, and
correspond with other doctors about patients, medical research, and professional associations. On advanced systems, described in Chapter Six, doctors
will be able to use their "Executive Stations" to read
their morning mail, send and receive memos and
collect telephone messages—all on their display
screens. Some physicians may use the word processor
to write articles for professional journals and to prepare speeches for seminars and professional conferences.

PERSONAL APPLICATIONS

Authors, writers, and professionals are switching to
word processors and finding, to their pleasure, that it
is revolutionizing the way they do their writing and
related tasks. More and more writers are discarding
their pencils and standard electric typewriters for
word processors. Novelists John Hersey and Richard
Condon, along with best selling luminaries, Michael
Crichton (*Congo*), Ernest Herbert (*Dogs of March*), and
Stanley Elkin (*The Living End*) use word processing
in their manuscript development.

Professor Elkin, who suffers from multiple scle-
rosis, praises his word processor. "You don't have to
screw around erasing and crossing out, finding a clear
place in the forest to drop the next hat. If I'd had it in
1964, I'd have written three more books by now."[1]

"After working on the word processor for 20
minutes, I knew it was going to change my life,"
Ernest Herbert said. "Once I learned it could do the
two essential things a writer really needs—insert and
delete—I knew I'd finally moved from the Stone Age
to the Space Age."[2]

[1]"Plugged-In Prose," *Time Magazine* (August 10, 1981), p. 68.
[2]Latamore, Berton, "A Fluid Well for Your Words," *Personal Computing* (January, 1983), p. 106.

Perhaps the most famous word processor user is former President, Jimmy Carter. Carter, who joins a growing number of writers using these electronic marvels, prepared the manuscript of his memoirs on the Lanier No-Problem word processor. Carter established a full writing/typing routine and made excellent progress in mastering the word processor's intricacies. "It's been surprisingly easy. Only a couple of times I've had to call Lanier and ask, 'How do I get out of this quandary?' " A second Lanier No-Problem unit has been used by Rosalyn to complete her book. Both machines were installed in the family study in Plains.

Multitalented stage and screen star, Raquel Welch, is writing an exercise and beauty tip book. She has acquired a word processor and is composing her thoughts by dictating into a tape recorder. Bo Derick and other celebrity-authors are taking to word processors in increasing numbers. The superstar of "10" fame has a "computer room" in her palatial California home where she keyboards her thoughts on an IBM Displaywriter.

FIGURE 5-4
Former President Jimmy Carter preparing the manuscript of his memoirs on the Lanier "No Problem" word processor at his home in Plains, Georgia. *Courtesy: Lanier*

Sesame Street consultant Christopher Cerf also praises his word processor. "I use my processor to write, to store notes, to create, to edit, to organize. It's already paid for itself. I don't need a secretary any more. It's the most important tool writers have been given since Gutenberg created movable type."[3]

Dr. Robert S. Eisenberg, chairman of the department of physiology at Rush University and an internationally known researcher in bioelectricity uses a word processor. (Bioelectricity is a branch of physiology that deals with the role of electricity in the function of cells and tissues.) Dr. Eisenberg feels that in scientific research, "output" means "words on paper—and that is where word processing comes in," Eisenberg said.

In the course of his work, Dr. Eisenberg writes about a hundred to two hundred pages a year of research reports, articles, and grant application reviews, as well as handling a fairly heavy correspondence. Prior to obtaining his word processor, he realized that he was using all the time of nearly two secretaries just to do his own writing. The Physiology Department now uses two word processors. One of the terminals is used by the department secretary during regular working hours, and by one or more of the faculty for writing after hours. The other terminal is kept in Eisenberg's own office and is used by him during daytime hours. After hours, it is typically used by a faculty member who may work until midnight composing his or her scientific reports.

OTHER WORD PROCESSING APPLICATIONS IN THE COLLEGE ENVIRONMENT

One of the frustrations that graduate students encounter when they are preparing for the final stages of their degree requirements is *writing the paper*. Often, this difficulty can be traced to a procedural problem and poor organization. Professors also share some of these writer frustrations in lack of time, poor organization, and the "publish or perish" syndrome that hangs over their heads.

[3]Ibid.

The writer can store research notes, by descriptors or glossary codes, in the word processor's memory bank. Then, when information is needed on any topic, it can be retrieved in its entirety for verification and/or inclusion. These codes replace the index cards created for file folders. Storing information electronically permits researchers to create their own individualized data banks during the data-gathering stage. This technique, together with the ease of editing and revising, is the key advantage cited by many writers that now use word processors.

Freelance Writers

Alvin Toffler used a word processor in completing his famous book, *The Third Wave.* He praises his word processor and the benefits derived from its increased speed, accuracy, and flexibility. He describes his experiences with a word processor in his book, *The Third Wave:*

> To learn how—and to speed up my own work—I bought a simple computer, used it as a word processor, and wrote the latter half of this book on it. To my pleasure, I found I could master the machine in a single short session. Within a few hours I was using it fluently. After more than a year at the keyboard I am still amazed by its speed and power.
>
> Today, instead of typing a draft of a chapter on paper, I type on a keyboard that stores it in electronic form on what is known as a "floppy disk." I see my words displayed before me on a TV-like screen. By punching a few keys I can instantly revise or rearrange what I have written, shifting paragraphs, deleting, inserting, underlining, until I have a version I like. This eliminates erasing, "whiting out," cutting, pasting, stripping, Xeroxing, or typing successive drafts. Once I have corrected the draft, I press a button, and a

Alvin Toffler. *Photo by: Susan Wood*

printer at my side makes a letter-perfect final copy for me at vision-blurring speeds.[4]

Isaac Asimov, science and science-fiction author, uses a Radio Shack TRS-80 Model II and the Scripsit word processing software program for his writing. "It's so easy," he says. "When an idea strikes, I head for my word processor. It's easy to compose, then edit what I write, because it's all done on the screen—electronically! When the story is just right, I print it—letter perfect—on my Daisy Wheel printer."

At first, Isaac Asimov was terrified of word processors. He trained on the vendor's audio cassette training course and reference manual and built up his confidence. Now all his writing is on a word processor. He enjoys the convenience of inserting, deleting, and moving material. "I can access almost any function with just a couple of keystrokes," explains Isaac. "If I don't like a word, sentence—even a whole page of copy—I just 'Zap' it away! And because all menus and prompts are displayed in plain language, I spend my time writing—not trying to memorize codes and commands."

Guy Tower, an independent consultant, associated with various divisions of the Chase Manhattan Bank, edits and writes articles and newsletters about international trade, financial analysis and feasibility studies related to industrial projects and international trade promotion activities.

Mr. Tower describes his involvement with word processors:

> After two years of intensive research, I was finally ready to put down in writing the results of my research. Because of the nature of my publication, I could not use a regular typewriter; each page was essentially composed of an association of rectangular boxes, each containing sets of various data for readers. Moreover, these boxes had to be regularly updated and shifted from one

[4]Toffler, Alvin, *The Third Wave*, p. 205.

chapter to another. Often, the data had to be completely disregarded and replaced with a new set of boxes. Using a regular typewriter would have been a nightmare of incredible proportions, and costs of new editing and publishing would have made the venture unprofitable.

I shopped around for about three full months to locate the appropriate equipment, harassing salesmen and technical people. My satisfaction was reached when I started working with a system that met my needs. There was no need to learn how to use the software; it took me about four hours to fully operate the machine, considering I had no previous experience with personal computers or word processors.

Now, thanks to my word processor, I am my own boss: I type the publication, edit it, publish it, send marketing letters (through List/Merging) in 35 countries worldwide, mail invoices, produce advertising material and adapt it to each environment, keep my financial records in order, all using my word processor. My wife, initially opposed to such an expensive purchase (another expensive toy!), now could not start her papers, always heavily edited at the last minute, unless she has my word processor under her command. Finally, to add a not-so-serious note, my three-year-old daughter enjoys inserting, deleting and drawing Christmas trees on the screen along with her name.

Robert Seward is an attorney who practices with his father and younger brother in Rockville Centre, New York. His law firm, Seward & Seward, was established in 1974, is involved in general law practice, and represents the Village of Rockville Centre. The village is in the heart of Nassau County and has a population of 28,000.

A friend introduced Bob to the IBM Displaywriter, and Bob was "sold" after his first demonstration. Prior to acquiring the Displaywriter, Bob did

FIGURE 5-5
Standard last will and testament from Displaywriter

<u>LAST WILL AND TESTAMENT</u>

-OF-

     I,   , residing at   ·   , County of Nassau and State of New York, do hereby make, publish and declare this to be my Last Will and Testament, hereby revoking any and all former Wills and Codicils by me at any time heretofore made.

<u>FIRST</u>
     I direct that all of my just debts, administration and funeral expenses be paid as soon after my death as may be practicable.

<u>SECOND</u>
     All the rest, residue and remainder of my property, whether real, personal or mixed and wheresoever situate, of which I may die seized or possessed, or in which I may any interest or over which I may have any power of appointment or testamentary disposition, including any lapsed dispositions, I give, devise, and bequeath to my beloved son,   to have and to hold the same, absolutely and forever.

<u>THIRD</u>
     I hereby nominate, constitute and appoint   as Executor of this my Last Will and Testament. In the event that he should fail to qualify or having qualified thereafter ceases to act as my Executor, then in such event, I nominate, constitute and appoint my husband,   as my substitute or successor Executor. Neither of the above named persons shall be required to give any bond or other security for the faithful performance of his duties in any jurisdiction.

     IN WITNESS WHEREOF, I have hereunto set my hand and seal this   day of March in the year One Thousand Nine Hundred Eighty Two.

     _____ (L.S.)

     The foregoing instrument was, on the day of the date thereof, signed, sealed, published and declared by   , the Testatrix therein named, as and for her Last Will and Testament, in the presence of us, who, at her request, in her presence, and in the presence of each other, have hereunto subscribed our names as witnesses.

_____ residing at_____

                              _____

_____residing at_____

                              _____

FIGURE 5-5

(cont.)

SURROGATE'S COURT: NASSAU COUNTY

--X
                                          :
In the Matter of the Application to   :   File No.
Determine the Estate Tax under Article 26:
of the Tax Law upon the Estate of   :
                                          :
                                          :   NOTICE OF MOTION
                                          :
                          Deceased.   :
                                          :
--X

S I R S :

          PLEASE TAKE NOTICE, that on the verified petition of

, dated the   day of , 1982, and on the supporting papers made

a part thereof, the petitioner will move at a Surrogate's Court

to be held in and for the County of Nassau, at the Surrogate's

Court Room, in the County of Nassau, on the   day of , 1982 at

10:00 o'clock in the forenoon of that day, or as soon thereafter

as counsel can be heard, for an order exempting the estate of

   , deceased, from the tax imposed by the article of the Tax

Law relating to tax on estates of deceased persons.

Dated: , 1982

                          Yours, etc.,

TO: ZOLA ARONSON, ESQ.
    114 Old Country Road
    Mineola, NY 11501

extensive revision work, making five or six revisions and meticulously reviewing each document. Now with initial keyboarding on the disk, making revisions is easy. "I can't imagine how we got along without one in our practice. It has made life so much more bearable." Since then, Bob has upgraded from a low-speed printer to a 60-cps printer. Speed is important in printing 70-page appeals, especially if you have to run off ten perfect copies.

Seward & Seward employs two secretaries on two IBM Displaywriters. Since IBM does not provide training with the Displaywriter, the secretaries had to "fend for themselves" trying to learn from the operator's manual. The real learning took place when they began actually keyboarding applications. Although Bob does not keyboard himself, he does know how to operate the system and often uses it after 5 P.M. when his secretaries leave for the day. He often calls up documents on the screen and does the revisions himself.

The primary applications for the Displaywriter that Bob's firm uses are real estate contracts, wills, briefs, and documents relating to the Village of Rockville Centre.

He keeps a standard will stored on disk. When a client requests his firm to prepare a will, doing so takes no more than 15 or 20 minutes. The names, addresses, and other variables are changed instantly, using the global search and replace feature of the Displaywriter. Ordinarily a will would take up to a week to be finalized and delivered to the client. An example of his standard will and a notice of motion document is shown in Figure 5–5. These items are stored on disk and are used frequently.

John Kirk, editor of *Inside Word Processing*, says:

> When I go to bed each night, I kneel down and say, "God bless mommy, and God bless daddy, and God Bless my Xerox 860!"
>
> My Xerox 860—with its full-page display, letter-quality printer, and dual-disk drives—has

totally changed my life as a self-employed professional writer. Nobody could ever force me to return to my standard electric typewriter—despite the fact that it is a fantastic typewriter that served me well for 15 years.

I do all of my writing on a screen—just as I'm doing this story. And I do most of my editing on the screen, too. However, since I have spent so many years—about 30—editing with a pencil on paper, I will print out at 500 words a minute (can you believe such a thing?) any serious writing and edit that hard copy with a pencil. Once I've finished editing, I then make the revisions electronically and print out the completed version, one, two, three—just like that.

If you rent or buy your own word processor, you'll discover that the old ways of thinking will disappear. But they disappear slowly. Here's an example of what I mean:

> Shortly after I'd gotten the hang of using the 860, I wrote and re-wrote and re-wrote a 19-page story for *Computer Decisions*, a great magazine. Finally, after several days of nit-picking my own work, I was satisfied, "That's it," I told myself. "No more revisions."

> Since it was 5:30 P.M. and I was tired, I told myself: "I'll type in the morning." Only then did it dawn on me that I didn't have to spend all of the next morning re-typing those 19 pages. Everything was in the system's memory.

> "Idiot," I said to myself, "you're into word processing!" I highlighted the story's title in the system's index, sent the story on to the printer and by 5:55 P.M. that night I had a beautifully-typed manuscript—a manuscript that I could never have duplicated with an electric typewriter, certainly not in terms of neatness. I went home still not quite believing that I had accomplished an entire morning's work in 20 minutes.

I also research and write a monthly newsletter called, *Inside Word Processing*. (See appendix section.) In the old days before word processing, I had a hell of a time turning out camera ready copy—i.e., four typed sheets that will be photographed by the offset printer and then printed. Do you know what it's like to proof such a page and discover a typo—one single letter that's wrong. I'd try to get the sheet back in the typewriter so I could strike over the letter—after I'd have to re-type the entire page. Typing with an electric typewriter is a sure *time killer*!!

Ya know, maybe at night I should say, "God bless my Xerox 860, God bless mommy, and God bless daddy."

Amy D. Wohl is the "Guru" of office automation and President of Advanced Office Concepts Corp., a leading office systems consulting firm based in Bala

FIGURE 5-6
John Kirk in his office

Cynwyd, Pennsylvania. In addition to on-site consulting, conducting seminars and being a guest speaker at numerous conferences, Amy edits and distributes a newsletter, *Advanced Office Concepts* (see appendix section).

For their multitask operation, Advanced Office Concepts uses a word processor. Amy says that she and her staff use their systems for literally everything from list management, text processing, calendaring, to printing labels.

Her most coveted use of the terminal (outside of text processing) is for electronic mail. Since she and her partner, Dr. Howard L. Morgan, spend 90 percent of their time away from the office and both keep a hectic intercontinental schedule, electronic mail is often the only real means of staying on top of business. By subscribing to a national network, Amy and her associates can speak to one another from almost anywhere in the world.

FIGURE 5-7
Amy D. Wohl and her partner, Dr. Howard L. Morgan, at one of their terminals

Plugging into "The Office of the Future" 6

Your word processor can represent a key component toward your quest for a complete integrated information system (IIS). Office systems vendors have the technology to combine computer technology with the evolving office systems environment, offering increased productivity and improved communications. Your word processor is capable of growing in many different ways to fit whatever field you're in. With thousands of ready-to-run application programs and hundreds of plug-in accessories, you and your information workers will be able to handle all kinds of information: words, numbers, images, and voice.

You can, for instance, combine word processing, data processing, telecommunications, and photo-typesetting on the same system. Modern desktop word processors or microcomputers can deliver far greater versatility, ease of operation and cost effectiveness than installing two, three, or even four different systems at one location.

Chapter Six will explore the strategy of integrat- **87**

ing your word processor with other technologies. These technologies follow naturally from the way people work in offices (and in some cases, homes). People use the spoken word, the written word, numbers, and pictures to communicate and assimilate information in a friendly, personable way. These forms of communication are integrated, often used simultaneously, and necessary for productive office work. We will explore how to use these technologies with our word processor, how to access, and how to apply them to our own tasks and activities. The first technology that you can combine with your word processor is data processing.

WORD PROCESSING/ DATA PROCESSING

Data processing is the most advanced and widely applied of the technologies. You can incorporate data processing functions into your word processor by combining BASIC language computing and sophisticated word processing. Mailing lists can be managed and merged for direct mail letters, or calculations can be made and inserted in a customized contract. All this can be done either from a single terminal or simultaneously from multiple terminals. Remote location can share the same capabilities through telecommunications.

Advanced software makes this merger possible. Data processing software enables you to write, edit, list, run, and store programs on your disk, as well as store, retrieve, and process data on disk. Through these DP/WP multifunctional capabilities, programs such as full business accounting, video spreadsheets, data management, and custom data processing applications written in almost any of the common computer languages can be achieved on your word processor.

Most word processing systems provide the BASIC language as it is the most common and easy-to-use computer language, allowing the user to write programs tailored to specific needs.

FIGURE 6-1
Integrating WP and DP. Basic Smart Disc Option for the EZ-1
word processor. This software option enables the user to write,
edit, list, run, and store programs, as well as store, retrieve, and
process data on disk. *Courtesy: Lanier*

To work effectively, you need timely, accurate, and
complete information. That is what an advanced electronic storage, retrieval, and communications system
gives you—the right information, at the right time,
and in the right place: your office or workstation.
With electronic filing capability, you spend less time
and energy struggling to find information, or struggling without it when you need it.

One implementation of file management at the
workstation level uses floppy disks rather than rigid
disks. But, through the use of a special internal or
rigid disk (explained in Chapter One), this high-
capacity electronic filing cabinet in your word processor eliminates the physical handling and switching
of diskettes. As a result, many operations are
simplified.

**RECORDS
MANAGEMENT
(ELECTRONIC
FILING CABINET)**

89

VISUALIZING A FILE MANAGEMENT CONCEPT

Electronically, filing can be accomplished through a hierarchical filing system through documents, folders, and drawers. A drawer corresponds to a floppy disk. On larger word processing systems, the drawers may be larger in capacity, and they are "contained" within named cabinets (disk drives) and file rooms (nodes in a future networked multisystem configuration).

Figure 6–2 illustrates a hierarchical filing system, from document to folder to drawer. On advanced systems, electronic filing allows users to:

1. View a "master directory" of all the documents in the folders within a drawer.
2. Flip (electronically) through the index of folders by pressing the cursor key. This "opens" the drawer to display an index of documents. To go a step further, when inside an index of document names, you can command a function key to take you back to the folder-level directory, and so on.

FIGURE 6-2
An electronic filing system. Even a single floppy disk allows users to organize documents into multiple "folders" on that floppy. Each floppy disk represents a "drawer."

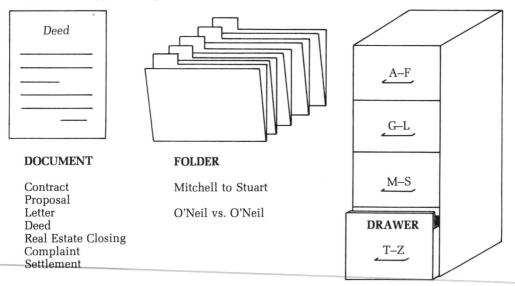

DOCUMENT	FOLDER
Contract	Mitchell to Stuart
Proposal	
Letter	O'Neil vs. O'Neil
Deed	
Real Estate Closing	
Complaint	
Settlement	

When you file a document, this special feature can automatically analyze it to find the key words that might be used to locate it after it's filed. Later on, you can retrieve it by simply keyboarding a few words contained in the material.

AUTOMATIC KEY WORD INDEXING

For example, an attorney might want to find all previous work done in his or her office on publishing contracts filed in the British West Indies in 1981 and 1982. He or she would keyboard "publishing, British West Indies, 1981 and 1982." Instantly, an index to the location of any electronic document containing all these words would be available for review on the screen.

More and more companies are merging their word processing and phototypesetting equipment to improve the flow of communications. By using your existing word processor terminal, you can discover a new way to combine the advantages of word processing and typesetting to save time and money and produce more professional-looking documents.

THE WORD PROCESSING CONNECTION IN PHOTO-TYPESETTING

Eliminate Redundant Keyboarding

The interface between word processing and phototypesetting equipment eliminates redundant keyboarding of information. Instead of rekeying information that has already been keyed on a word processor, the phototypesetting operator can transfer the information already recorded on the word processor into the phototypesetter. This one-time keyboarding and proofreading saves up to 50 percent of the costs for the labor of keyboarding and reproofreading the text that has already been typed.

How It Works

All you have to do is type, revise, and perfect your copy on your word processor. While typing, you must insert instructions (or special codes) that inform the 91 typesetter of such things as the size of characters (type size) and the amount of space between the lines (leading).

If you keyboard information to be processed and printed out on word processors, you do not have to insert these instructions. If you keyboard material onto word processing equipment to be printed out onto phototypesetting equipment, you must insert the special typesetting codes where they are needed if you know them. If you do not know these codes, you must alert the typesetter by inserting a symbol on the copy wherever a typesetting code is required. This is a cooperative effort between the word processor operator and the typesetter. The typesetter, when he or she receives your copy, must go back and replace the symbols with the proper codes. This method frees the person who operates the word processing equipment from having to learn typesetting codes.

The original copy is typed on the word processor and recorded on a magnetic disk. A typed printout can be produced on the printer for proofreading. The recorded copy is then corrected on the word processor. Little time and small effort are expended because all the keystrokes have been captured.

Set Type Automatically

When the copy is final, it is a simple matter to go from the word processor to typeset output. Most word processors are disk-compatible and can act as off-line terminals for typesetting systems. This is an enormous advantage, because many companies can reap substantial savings in printing costs by converting data into compact, attractive forms—a very important factor when documents must be distributed to a large audience.

An advertisement for Quadex Composition Systems demonstrates how typesetting reduces the cost of producing corporate publications by reducing the amount of space required for text. A paperback copy of *War and Peace* is compared with a printed "manuscript" version of the translated novel. (See Figure 6–3.) Another, more vivid example of how photocomposition improves the quality and condenses written communications appears in the comparative pages of Figures 6–4 and 6–5.

FIGURE 6-3
The effects of typesetting on *War and Peace. Courtesy:* Compugraphic

THE EFFECTS OF TYPESETTING ON WAR AND PEACE

"MANUSCRIPT"
Paper Cost: $10.01 per copy
Shipping Weight: 18.72 lbs.
Storage Space: 432.87 cu. ft.
(per 1,000 copies)
Pages: 1,933
(printed one side–8½" × 11")

TYPESET BOOK
Paper Cost: $1.11 per copy
Shipping Weight: 1.13 lbs.
Storage Space: 30.13 cu. ft.
(per 1,000 copies)
Pages: 1,456
(printed 2 sides–4⅛" × 7")

Quadex Composition Systems

Would you force your customers, sales personnel, and other employees to read *War and Peace* in typewritten manuscript form?

You may be doing that right now.

Your company may publish far more words *per month* than you'll find in Tolstoy's great epic . . . in a bulky typewritten format that costs more to print, ship, and store than publications set in type.

There's a way out of this cost crunch: a Quadex Composition System. An easy-to-use, modular

system that turns just plain data into attractive, compact information.

Find out how Quadex Composition Systems can help you win the war on words and enjoy more peace of mind at budget time.

For more information, write or call now.

 **compugraphic**
Compugraphic Corporation
200 Ballardvale Street
Wilmington, Massachusetts 01887
(617) 944-6555, ext. 2911

FIGURE 6-4
The typed copy

HOW PHOTOCOMPOSITION FITS INTO THE
"OFFICE OF THE FUTURE"

THE "OFFICE OF THE FUTURE" CONCEPT

The "Office of the Future" concept is awakening computer manufacturers to the fact that their products that support the office environment will now be more carefully assessed by prospective buyers as to how these products contribute to this concept and profits.

One area being affected by office automation is photocomposition. To help clarify this issue, Compugraphic Corporation, the leader in the photocomposition industry, has accepted the challenge of defining where and how phototypesetting fits into the profit picture.

At one time photocomposition was viewed as an art or creative function which does not lend itself to standardization or production measurements, or as a function that should be in the basement with the printing press. But not with today's technology. Photocomposition is now viewed as a part of the modern, automated office environment.

Decision makers need to be made aware of how phototypesetting fits into today's computerized offices. Compugraphic has designed an effective consulting program. It is called <u>MAP</u>, <u>Management Audit for Productivity</u>, and it puts photocomposition in perspective with the "Office of the Future." <u>MAP</u> is a program that provides a consulting service which would normally cost thousands of dollars. The service is analytical in nature and zeros in on the roots of the office productivity issue. It is an audit of composition productivity for management and is offered by Compugraphic, a company with over ten years experience in the industry.

TOP MANAGEMENT AWARENESS

The <u>MAP</u> program is designed to seek top management's commitment to perform a professional, quantified analysis study of the text composition handling capabilities of their organization and provide information for management to evaluate the potential role photocomposition can play within their automated office. The basic objective of the Management Audit for Productivity (<u>MAP</u>) is to:

A. Analyze the profitable opportunities for photocomposition within a company.

B. Compare applications to developed productivity benchmarks and to determine production standards per job.

HOW PHOTOCOMPOSITION FITS INTO THE "OFFICE OF THE FUTURE"

THE "OFFICE OF THE FUTURE" CONCEPT

The "Office of the Future" concept is awakening computer manufacturers to the fact that their products that support the office environment will now be more carefully assessed by prospective buyers as to how these products contribute to this concept and profits.

One area being affected by office automation is photocomposition. To help clarify this issue, Compugraphic, the leader in the photocomposition industry, has accepted the challenge of defining where and how phototypesetting fits into the profit picture.

At one time photocomposition was viewed as an art or creative function which does not lend itself to standardization or production measurements, or as a function that should be in the basement with the printing press. But not with today's technology. Photocomposition is now viewed as a part of the modern, automated office environment.

Decision makers need to be made aware of how phototypesetting fits into today's computerized offices. Compugraphic has designed an effective consulting program. It is called **MAP**, *Management Audit for Productivity*, and it puts photocomposition in perspective with the "Office of the Future." **MAP** is a program that provides a consulting service which would normally cost thousands of dollars. The service is analytical in nature and zeros in on the roots of the office productivity issue. It is an audit of composition productivity for management and is offered by Compugraphic, a company with over ten years experience in the industry.

TOP MANAGEMENT AWARENESS

The **MAP** program is designed to seek top management's commitment to perform a professional, quantified analysis study of the text composition handling capabilities of their organization and provide information for management to evaluate the potential role photocomposition can play within their automated office. The basic objective of the Management Audit for Productivity (**MAP**) is to:

A. Analyze the profitable opportunities for photocomposition within a company.

B. Compare applications to develop productivity benchmarks and to determine production standards per job.

C. Determine production complexity, frequency, printing run, average production time and deadline period for all applications.

D. Provide a summary of all applications, estimated production time and costs.

E. Establish a system overhead rate for calculating cost savings and production capabilities.

F. Analyze peak periods based on the highest concentration of jobs in a pre-determined period of time.

G. Propose equipment configurations that will meet production requirements.

H. Schedule implementation support programs for training, service and user consultations to insure the installation will be profitable.

The **MAP** audit is a fact-finding project used to assist in the evaluation of profitability in office photocomposition. It can have a significant impact on how any company views its present and future publication producing capabilities.

THE IMPACT OF MAP

As mentioned earlier, manufacturers of computer systems are concerned about the methods that will be used by a business to assess the strengths of their products. These methods, and subsequent decisions, hold the key to the successful use of a company's human resources as well as the success of a manufacturer's systems.

One thing we all know about the American business man is that the decisions that will be made in this or any other area will be grounded in hard, analytical cost-benefit data. Since the data processing revolution, the business of doing business has become increasingly statistical.

Computer modeling, forecasting, analyzing, scrutinizing are now a course of discussion in any business school worth its salt, and more than just discussion in any large business enterprise. As a matter of fact, the vendor of any large, multi-product line of computer systems, whether they be for office or manufacturing use, has had to learn a completely new language and develop a new set of sales skills to even be considered as a valued supplier. We have to be concerned with the prospect's profit picture.

PHOTOCOMPOSED PAGE
OVER TWICE
AS MUCH COPY
PLUS QUALITY

FIGURE 6-5
The typeset copy. Reprint of advertisement: *Courtesy: Compugraphic*

FIGURE 6-6
MCS photocomposition system. *Courtesy: Compugraphic*

If your word processor is located far from the typesetter, you'll gain more time with installing a special communications option. Copy can be transmitted over phone lines from your word processor directly into your phototypesetter. No time is lost for the delivery of the manuscript or the disks. The word processing–phototypesetting interface is a practical way to expand your service and offer professional-looking documents easily, quickly, and economically.

COMMUNICATIONS CAPABILITY

FIGURE 6-7
Varityper's Comp/Set: At the left, an off-line editing terminal; on the right, a phototypesetter shown with modem for telecommunications option. *Courtesy: AM International*

Overnight express service works well, if you don't mind waiting overnight. But if you have to get written or graphic information somewhere in a few hours—or as little as one minute—electronic mail works much better. The electronic mail capability puts instant electronic communications at your fingertips. You can send messages almost anywhere in seconds. Right from your desk. Simply insert your document into a telecopier terminal, pick up your phone, and dial. In less time than it takes a courier to appear at your office, a crisp, clear copy of what you've just sent will appear in another terminal cross-town, cross-country, even cross-ocean. In just two to six minutes, facsimile or telecopier terminals can transmit a page to any of the tens of thousands of other terminals around the world.

FIGURE 6-8
Communicating word processors/personal computers. *Courtesy:*
Tymnet

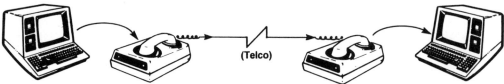

(Telco)

Your word processor can be equipped with a modem, and you can transmit documents from one word processor to another. This technology is referred to as "communicating word processors." Its costs are competitive with conventional slower methods. For example, your word processor can send a three-page letter across the country in less than one minute, for less than 40 cents, at current after-hours phone rates. And there are no delays for posting or mailing. Simply type a letter at your desk and indicate its destination. Your word processor does the rest automatically. For large documents, electronic mail is substantially less expensive than couriers or facsimiles. And much more convenient.

Electronic In-Baskets

Usually if your word processor has an electronic mail system feature, it is likely to have an electronic "in-basket" feature. This is an automatic summary of all the letters, memos, and other communications that have come in during the day. At the touch of a button, you can find out what's in *your* in-basket: subject, sender, date received, and date reply needed. You can choose to look at your mail any time you wish: first thing in the morning, between meetings, after hours. And you can look at either a listing of your messages or the actual message.

In addition, an electronic mail feature can include an *electronic buck-slip.* Users can review a document, add some notes, and pass it on, with notes, to someone else for action. That's an electronic way of "passing the buck!"

OCR stands for optical character recognition. It is the ability to read written, typewritten, or other printed material directly from the source and then transfer its

OCR

FIGURE 6-9
By means of optical character recognition (OCR) technology, the DEST Workless station enters text from typewritten pages into most popular word processors in 25 seconds. It reads copies as well as originals, typed in any of eight common typestyles. The text is converted into electronic signals, which are fed into the word processing system for later retrieval. *Courtesy: Dest Corp.*

contents to a word processor, a computer, or a variety of other devices. An OCR unit—sometimes called a page reader or page scanner—can read text typed on standard office typewriters and send that text directly to your word processing system, without you or your operator having to type the text again to enter it into the word processing system. In the world of data processing, OCR has been an accepted, widely used tool for more than 25 years. Now the word processing world is discovering the power of OCR when added to your word processing system.

The Benefits

When you add OCR to your word processing system, you extend the power of your WP operation to every typewriter throughout your entire organization. Just as the concept of distributed data processing has changed the nature of computing, the concept of distributed word processing can change the nature of word processing in your organization.

With OCR, every standard single-element typewriter in your organization can input directly to your word processor. Or, looking at it another way, every typist in your office can become an effective part of your word processing operation. Every typewriter in your office can function as an off-line word processing terminal for text entry.

How OCR Is Used in Word Processing

Figure 6–10 illustrates how OCR works with a word processing system—the typical copy flow for documents that are reviewed and edited. This flow can be altered for different applications, and, for some work, direct input on the word processor still may be desirable. For most work, the basic steps are:

1. Author generates original document by longhand or dictation.

FIGURE 6-10
The OCR process

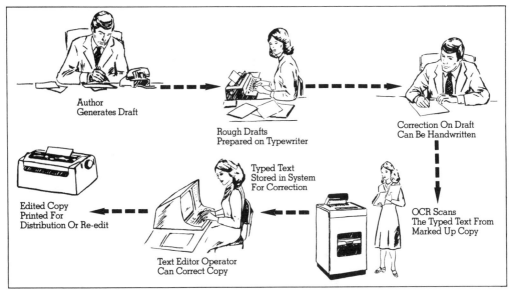

2. Secretary keyboards a draft of document on standard office typewriter.

3. Author reviews and marks changes on the draft with a special felt-tip pen (red).

4. Marked-up draft is scanned by OCR.

5. Word processor operator edits the document by referencing the marked-up draft.

6. Corrected document is then printed out.

The Future of OCR

As word processors become a fixture on every desk in the office, as intelligent workstations for managers, professionals, and support staff become commonplace, and as the cost of these word processors and workstations begins to approach the cost of standard typewriters, the economic need for today's OCR equipment will begin to fade. When this occurs, there will not be any rekeyboarding. Document preparation will be done directly on a terminal by the originator of the document.

FIGURE 6-11
OFIS reader 1240 OCR page reader. *Courtesy: Burroughs*

FIGURE 6-12
Hendrix TeleTypereader OCR system for up to ten-fold
improvement in message preparation efficiency. *Courtesy:
Hendrix*

The next generation of OCR devices will go far beyond their present capabilities. New systems will prepare messages up to ten times faster than an operator keyboarding at a terminal, resulting in lower labor costs, shorter message preparation time, and peak-period volume efficiency. Some of these improved systems are currently being introduced to offices right now. (See Figure 6–12.)

NETWORKS

Ultimately, every machine in an office that works with information will have the built-in ability to interconnect with a telecommunications *network*. A *network* can be defined as a linked system of terminals that can operate independently, yet permit a combination of two or more to share data and other information. From a user's point of view, typing into the network will provide access to information stored in the form of data on computers, text on word processors, images on microfilm, and voice on the network itself.

Xerox's well advertised Ethernet has garnered some support from outside vendors that perceive a market in offering devices that will hook up to such nets. Wang has established their own version called Wangnet. This local networking scheme uses some frequencies of a coaxial cable to shuttle communications between Wang devices, and it makes other frequencies available for other types of transmission, such as video, data, or voice. The telecommunication network is seen as the key in the office automation evolution. (See Figure 6–13.)

There are a variety of choices for word processor users and for those planning business information systems. Networks can be used to manage the complexity of volumes of information.

The AT&T subsidiary—American Bell—offers their Advanced Information Systems (AIS) Net 1 Service that links different computers, word processors and data networks. This network features distributed

FIGURE 6-13
Wang office automation evolution. *Courtesy: Wang Laboratories*

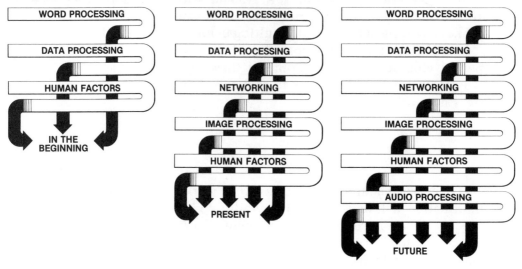

intelligent service, which means that it will be available throughout the country. It adds function and capability to existing terminals and word processors by providing users with the ability to design and control their own integrated system. With the American Bell Network system, you do not have to lay out a large sum of cash. You pay only for what you use.

Advantages of Networks to Word Processor Users

1. Increased productivity by integrating diverse business systems and hardware.
2. Opening up of channels of communications between companies.
3. More timely communications using electronic message distribution and storage.
4. Wide range of applications, such as order entry from supplier to manufacturer to distributor, or claims processing between insurance agents and their carriers.
5. Provides expansion to accommodate a variety of additional functions.

For word processor users, networks provide an opportunity for one terminal to talk to another, whether it is across the country or across the room. While American Bell is concentrating on long-distance operations, other firms are trying to develop their own local networking systems.

Connecting dissimilar word processors and other electronic office devices creates a problem of communication incompatibility. Just imagine if your word processor could communicate with another word processor or terminal over an ordinary telephone line. Making the connection compatible, however, are special systems known as "black boxes."

BLACK BOXES: THE COMPATIBLE CONNECTORS!

"All right, you two . . . shake hands and start communicating."

Courtesy: Word Processing & Information Systems (July 1981).

FIGURE 6-14
Envax 500. Adding ENVAX to a word processor enables it to perform a variety of functions: doubling as a computer terminal for data entry or data base inquiry, sending typeset output to a remote location where the information will be automatically typeset, sending legal documents rapidly across country, transmitting properly formatted messages into the Telex and TWX networks, and general word processor communication. *Courtesy: Envax Corp.*

These intelligent microprocessor-based devices are programmed to handle a wide variety of equipment and make them compatible for communications. There are a variety of such devices, and they fall into the following categories:

1. *Protocol Translators*—These microprocessor-based machines translate communications codes and protocols into characters that are compatible for communications.

2. *Modems*—Also known as acoustic couplers, these are the primary tools in electronic mail and communicating word processors. Their function is to convert digital data into analog form and back again, thus enabling word processors and remote computers to communicate over ordinary telephone lines.

3. *Interfaces*—A type of "black box" device for the single purpose of interfacing word processors with peripheral devices and services.

4. *Port Extenders*—Port extenders are like multiple electric sockets. These devices can turn a machine's single communication outlet into dual or triple channels, making it possible for the machine to be interfaced with several devices.

Finally, when we talk about compatibility within different word processing systems, we really mean full *editability*. We want to know if we can write a file on our XYZ word processor, send it to another system for editorial revisions, and then have it sent back to us for further revisions. Eventually, we hope to have an agreed-upon text that can be printed.

Wohl says that multivendor environments offer very little full compatibility. She further cautions that, when you consider purchasing "black boxes" or other devices that promise to link up dissimilar pieces of equipment, you should apply a true check to whatever you read, see, or hear about compatibility. Says Wohl:

> Remember a principle from business law: Oral statements made by salesmen in pursuit of sales are not legally binding.[1]

CALENDAR MANAGEMENT

A word processor can even handle your scheduling and appointments. At a glance you can find out the day's appointments, the first available hour-long block of time, court docket schedules, or whatever calendar information you need. It can monitor follow-up dates and automatically remind you of key events. This is particularly useful for tickler files, docket control, and scheduling follow-up items.

INFORMATION BANKS

Electronic information banks enable the word processor or terminal owner to access information by subscribing to information services. By simply dialing an

---

[1]*Inside Word Processing*, a publication of Buyers Laboratory, Inc. (July, 1982), p. 4.

access number and keying in a personal identification code, subscribers can use their word processors to gain access to hundreds of data bases. Subscribers can also send messages to one another.

Attorneys can now search and locate citations and histories on every case from a lower court decision to a U.S. Supreme Court mandate by subscribing to one of the several legal data bases now available. In the medical field, data bases provide information on the most recent discoveries in cancer, blood, and heart research. Those in agribusiness can use data bases to check on the commodities market, to get weather reports, and to compute loan and depreciation schedules.

Currently, these information services are relatively expensive, and users must seriously evaluate

their needs before contracting with an information

service. The big drawback, of course, is the fee. While you are watching the data move across your terminal screen, you will be paying as much as a dollar a minute for the privilege. Table 6–1 has examples of information bank services. Response time is another key factor in considering subscribing to an information bank. Response time should be virtually instantaneous (maximum of 15 seconds).

Brief Summary of Information Bank Services

- *Management Contents (a Ziff Davis Subsidiary)*—has an on-line service that abstracts the magazines available via The Source. The fee is $35 an hour.
- *The Yankee Group (Yankee Net)*—combines electronic mail and computer conferencing that features research in advanced information technology. $10,000 to $17,000 per year.
- *The American Medical Association*—in combination with Telenet provides computerized medical data bases for hospitals and physicians.

TABLE 6–1
Data Bank Subscription Services

NAME OF SERVICE	SIGN-UP FEE	HOURLY RATES & OTHER FEES	TYPES OF SERVICES
CompuServe	None	22.50 (5 A.M. to 6 P.M. M–F) 5.00 (6 P.M.–5 A.M.)	Electronic newspapers; Personal computing; E-Mail; Bulletin boards; Games; On-line newsletters
Dow Jones News Retrieval Service "A Service"	None	40. (6 A.M.–6 P.M.) 12. (6 P.M.–6 A.M.) (plus $50 year)	Stock quotes; Wall St. Journal highlights; Corporate disclosures; Business, Financial information, Wire Service
DJ "B Service"	$25	60. (6 A.M.–6 P.M.) 12. (6 P.M.–6 A.M.)	
EIES Network	None	7.50 (all hrs) (plus $74/mth)	E-Mail; Computer-based conferencing; Information Exchange
The Source Telecomputing	$100	18. (7 A.M.–6 P.M. M–F) 5.75 (6 P.M.–12 A.M.) 4.25 (12 A.M.–7 A.M.)	General, Business, Financial, Airline schedules; E-Mail; Computing games; Entertainment

- *Metpath*—operates a large clinical laboratory and physicians subscribing to this service may access their test results on their terminal overnight. Metpath provides expanded service for doctors to access drug interaction data, financial management services, stock quotes (an item of interest to most physicians), and computerized games.
- *Lexis*—provides legal information services for the legal profession.
- *NewsNet*—is an electronic library of newsletters serving business, finance, technology, and government. A list of some of the newsletters provided by this service appears in Table 6–2.

Dow Jones News/Retrieval Service

This is perhaps the broadest, most comprehensive data base of any business news system. It includes:

- Up-to-the-minute news from Dow Jones domestic and international newswires.

TABLE 6–2
Electronic Newsletter Editions*

Advanced Office Concepts	Telecommunications Reports
Africa News Services	The Corporate Shareholder
Alexander Research & Communications	Ford Value Report
Ammard Publications	Education Funding News
Anderson Publishing	Fibre Optics & Communications
Arien Communications	The Energy Daily
Alcom	Online Database Report
Behavior Today	IRS Practices & Procedures
Marriage & Divorce Today	Research Monitor News
Sexually Today	Coal Outlook
Business Publishers	CableNews
Air/Water Pollution Report	RadioNews
Clean Water Report	VideoNews
Ecology USA	Satellite News
Fair Employment Report	The Photoletter
Federal Contract Opportunities	Television Digest
Handicapped Rights & Regulations	
Hazardous Waste News	

*Partial list.

FIGURE 6-16
Videotex® two-way information retrieval system. *Courtesy: Radio Shack Corp.*

- Articles from *The Wall Street Journal.*
- In-depth financial analysis of companies and industries from *Barron's.*
- Current day and historical quotations from the four major stock exchanges and the national OTC market, throughout the day, including volume, opening and closing prices, and highs and lows for the day.
- Selected business items from *The New York Times.*

Let's say you're looking for a fast-breaking story about the EXXON Corporation. Step-by-step, here's how to find it:

Step 1. Link up to the data bank.

Step 2. Punch XON (the stock symbol) to access EXXON HEADLINES.

Step 3. Punch the two buttons that identify the story you want, and call up the whole text.

TELECOMMUTING Up until now, all keyboarding and information processing tasks had to be done in an "office" where work space is expensive and where a quality staff is sometimes difficult to maintain. A new pattern of work has emerged where employees work at home instead of in an office. Home-work had its roots among blue-collar workers in the early twentieth century. It attracted garment workers, many of them illegal aliens. But this pattern has now spread to legal home-work programs for office workers and clerical staff. For homemakers with small children to care for, professionals, and others attracted to this form of work, home-work will increase within the next several years. Home-work will eventually affect our daily lives—especially with the proliferation of advanced information processing equipment. Alvin Toffler predicts that more and more workers will be linked to

FIGURE 6-17
Lanier commuting dictation system combined with No-Problem word processor being used at home by information worker. *Courtesy: Lanier*

their employers through electronics, creating "electronic cottages" from which people can work at home.

Inflation, commuting time, energy crises, and other external frustrations make commuting to a work environment unattractive to a growing number of potentially valuable personnel. In addition, the price of choice office space in central cities is skyrocketing. Other office costs of heating, lighting, and supplies can force some companies to employ fewer workers than is desirable. These factors are prompting corporations to rethink the ways and places in which information workers do their jobs. A new concept— "Telecommuting"—is slowly being implemented by some organizations. This idea allows information workers to perform some or all of their work at home or in mini-offices that are more convenient to the worker. Experts predict that as many as 15,000,000 workers could be earning their primary income from so-called home-work by the mid-1990s.

Many vendors have introduced product lines that provide word processing, sophisticated data processing, electronic mail, voice stored-and-forward processing, and other advanced features that will help to ease the home-office linkup. Lanier uses Telestaff, its home-site or satellite transcription system. The Telestaff allows transcription to be done in the home, in another office, or in any location where there is a telephone, combining the latest technology with a very practical design.

It is important to realize that some workers find telecommuting an ideal situation. Parents of young children (as pictured in Figure 6–17), who cannot find suitable baby sitters or day-care centers, are compelled to stay at home. Telecommuting offers them a chance to earn money at home. But not everyone may wish to participate in stay-at-home work. We discussed telecommuting in our word processing class at Nassau Community College. One of our students is disabled and confined to a wheelchair. When I mentioned telecommuting as an alternate work choice, she responded, "I don't want to stay at home,

Professor Rosen. I want to wake up in the morning, put on a pretty dress, travel to an office, and work with and be surrounded by people." Telecommuting is, however, ideal for security brokers and commodity traders who work almost exclusively out of their homes because much of their business is conducted over telephones and terminals connected to a variety of electronic information services. Home-site work environments open up exciting possibilities to other professionals such as editors, programmers, accountants, and writers, who can work for days without direct contact with the home office.

Telecommuting by Satellite Transmission

Another aspect of telecommuting makes use of high-speed facsimile or compressed audio tape transmission of word processing keyboarding by skilled and experienced personnel in remote locations of the

FIGURE 6-18
FAX-CAP Service. *Courtesy: Satellite Data Corp.*

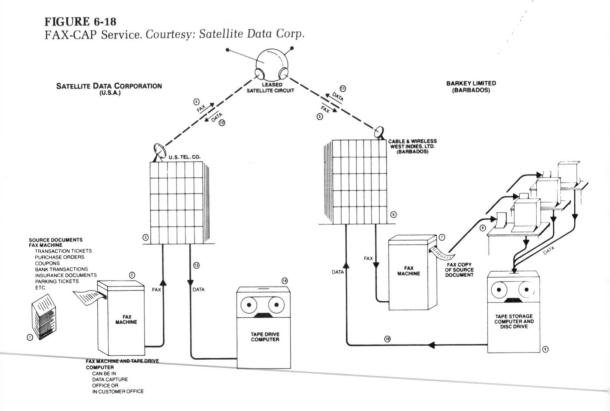

world. Quick data return via satellite is being offered to high-volume organizations and users by Satellite Data Corporation and its Barbados affiliate, Barkey, Ltd.

It is a way to import scarce keyboarding "labor" without immigration problems. With the new technology, organizations are relieved of the delays and errors caused by too few or unskilled data entry personnel. At the same time it opens the prospect of providing well paying work for English-speaking, literate West Indians. Inexpensive communications can help provide low-cost data entry for U.S. organizations, as well as improve the stability of the other countries. A diagram of telecommuting by Satellite Data Corporation Barbados connection appears in Figure 6–18.

VOICE MAIL

"I'm sorry, but she's not at her desk right now. May I take a message?" With this common phrase begins yet another round of "telephone tag"—a frustrating, time-consuming, and expensive exercise in missed phone calls that hampers the flow of business information and cuts down on the productivity of information professionals. In order to improve such vital day-to-day communications, voice mail or voice record, store, and forward technology addresses this problem. Voice mail can be interfaced with your word processor or terminal. It can be used from a pay phone, from home, or from work—through a conventional tone-generating telephone, or through dial phones equipped with commercially available tone-generating attachments.

Voice-Phone Helps Solve
Geographical Time Zone Problems

A cross-country flight is delayed, and an executive arrives in Oregon well after the Boston office closes.

Needing to get and to give information and messages immediately, the manager calls the Boston office from an airport pay phone, uses a security password, and listens to the confidential messages. The executive can either leave those messages in storage, record a verbal response, or edit the information and send it on to others with verbal annotations. The caller can also record messages and have the voice mail system automatically deliver them to the several managers, even if they are in different cities. No secretarial help is required, and the information is available to those designated whenever they choose to call into the system. But it remains confidential. Since names are used as identifiers, there is no need to remember long lists of telephone numbers or numeric codes.

In another example of voice-phone technology—two executives are traveling separately or are tied up in different meetings. Yet they must exchange vital information. That situation can lead to an entire day of "telephone tag." With voice-phone technology, confidential messages can be left, retrieved, and responded to at either executive's convenience.

Finally, an executive at home needs to keep up with office correspondence. By means of periodic calls to the voice mail system, the executive can wrap up work on the phone from home, selecting the order of priority of the messages.

How It Works—Technically!

Voice record, store, and forward technology digitizes voice messages and stores them on disks attached to a preprogrammed computer. It can be used from any phone equipped with conventional tone-generating attachment. The computer converts—or digitizes—voice tones into electronic impulses that are stored on magnetic disks. It then converts those impulses back into voice tones when the message is retrieved. The digitized messages retain the identity and even the voice inflections of the user.

FIGURE 6-19
Digital voice message systems

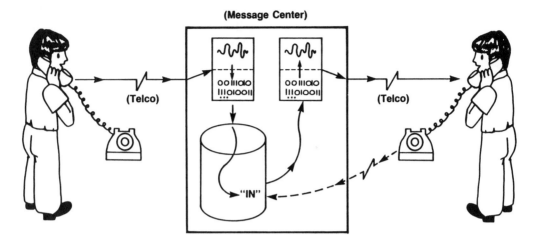

In this incredible shrinking world, communication has never been as important as it is right now. Traditional markets are being shattered and reformed. Barriers—national and cultural—are crumbling. Time itself is in a new context with incredible amounts of information available in tiny fractions of a second. The whole world is being compressed.

This compression leads to increased trade and commerce. As the world comes closer together, one major obstacle to continued growth of international trade is the language barrier. The application of new technology through language processing systems is revolutionizing language translation, both in terms of translation quality and man hours required. One of the leaders of this technology is ALSP—Automated Language Processing Systems—a Utah-based company which designs and simplifies translation and other text processing applications. Advanced systems are becoming refined to the point of representing languages according to their precise structural patterns.

Where does the human translator fit in? Language processing systems are not designed to replace

LANGUAGE PROCESSING SYSTEMS

115

the human translator. A good multilingual system, such as ALPS, complements the human translator who controls the quality of the text from start to finish. The result is a blend of man and machine that operates with extraordinary effectiveness.

How the ALPS Computer Translation System Works

The computer aids the human translator in several processing tasks. It:

1. automatically looks up the words, in each sentence, in its dictionary, which the translator can expand at any time;
2. presents on the screen words and phrases with more than one translation option, so that the translator can select the best one;
3. asks the translator questions about sentence structure to help produce grammatically correct sentences;

FIGURE 6-20
The multilingual system. *Courtesy: ALPS*

4. processes inflections, agreement, and ordering of words, based on the responses of the translator;

5. displays concurrently both the source text and the translation for ease of editing by the translator, who does the final editing and polishing of the translation. The translator can move, insert, delete, and edit words and phrases with a few keystrokes, often without retyping, until satisfied with the translation.

Interface Language Processing Systems with Your Word Processor

Language Processing systems, such as the ALPS system, can interface with your word processor to get the source text into the system and to get the translated material out in the desired form. The ALPS language processing system can receive text from another computer, from mag tape, from a variety of word processors, or via optical character recognition (OCR). Or the text can be typed in at the terminal if necessary. The ALPS computer translation system can output translated material to another computer, to a printer, onto mag tape, or to a variety of typesetting and phototypesetting equipment. For more information on language processing systems, contact:

> Automated Language Processing Systems—
> ALPS
> 190 West 800 North
> Provo, Utah 84601

At present, hundreds of electronic clearinghouses around the country provide word processing and personal computer operators with the means to scan messages posted by other users and to write in messages of their own. All they need is a word processing or computer terminal, a modem (a device to hook it up

ELECTRONIC BULLETIN BOARDS

to a telephone line), and the appropriate software. Bulletin board operators say the software and the needed telephone modem cost about $750.

Some bulletin boards specialize in art and antiques, and others carry detailed reports about computer software. Electronic bulletin boards are run by hobbyists and are accessible to anyone with the right phone number. Others, however, are open only to paying subscribers.

Care, Maintenance, and Service 7

If a problem arises while you are in the middle of keyboarding a document, you can take a series of logical steps to solve the problem:

PROBLEM ANALYSIS

1. Ask yourself the questions: What operation was I trying to perform when the problem occurred? Is this a malfunction of equipment or a procedural problem?

2. If it is a procedural problem, did you accomplish all the steps for that operation?

3. Review the steps. Have you left anything out?

4. If the answer is yes, clear the screen and begin the operation again.

5. If the answer is no, could it be a mechanical problem with the equipment? Is the equipment functioning properly? Where did you actually see the problem occurring? Was it the printer, the screen, the windows, the cursor position windows, or any of the prompt keys on the screen?

" . . . You'll be able to figure out the problem soon, ma'am.
John's bringing in the reference manuals."

Courtesy: Word Processing & Information Systems (April 1982).

6. If there are any special prompts or diagnostics that appear on your screen, refer to your operator's manual for the solution. For instance, if the prompt says, "DISK FULL," you may have to take the step of deleting or archiving documents from the disk for additional storage space. Or if the screen prompt says "CHECK PRINTER," you might find that you have run out of ribbon.

7. Check the following simple points such as:

Is the power on?

Is the terminal plugged in?

Is there a disk in the disk drive?

If these steps do not produce a solution, then go on to the next series of steps:

1. Check with your supervisor or co-worker. Often, they may have experienced a similar problem with a particular document application or system feature and know a solution or suggestion that may not be included in the operator's manual. Or they may point out that the step appears in a special section or heading of the manual that you would not normally look for.

2. If all else fails, telephone your support representative. Often, these reps can give you the solution over the phone.

Preventive maintenance can alleviate costly downtime. By carefully reading the special section in your operator's manual and following a prescribed preventive maintenance schedule, you can keep your system operating continuously. Included in most manuals is a chart or table of troubleshooting or problem-solving aids. The page may be divided into two columns and may look like the sample below:

Trouble-Shooting Guidelines

PROBLEM	*SOLUTION*
The cursor does not appear within 30 seconds after you press the power on button.	Turn the contrast (or bright) knob all the way to the right to insure maximum illumination on the screen.
	or
	Make sure the power plug is plugged in securely.

In another manual the page's format might be:

WHAT TO DO WHEN

If your printer malfunctions, follow the checklist below before calling your customer service representative:

- Is the microprocessor turned on?
- Check the cover for proper alignment. Your printer will not function if the cover is off or not securely fastened.
- Check the ribbon. Some models are equipped to shut off when end-of-ribbon is detected.
- Make sure the text on your screen is memorized, remove the disk, then turn the microprocessor off for a moment or two. This resets the printer and may cure the problem. If this occurs frequently, call your service technician.

- Remove the cover and check the carriage guide rails for a blockage.
- Press down on the "C" button on the carriage locking lever to make sure it is seated properly.
- If your print quality is poor, check the printwheel for wear and clogging.
- Check the cables on the back of the printer for proper connection.

PREVENTIVE CARE

Electrical Power

1. Check to see that the power cord is secure in the socket at the beginning of every day.
2. Use the proper sequence to turn your system on. Some systems specify that you turn the microprocessor on first, wait for a warm-up period, and then turn your terminal on.
3. Discourage office personnel and cleaning crews from disconnecting the terminal or microprocessor or from moving the equipment from place to place.

External Surfaces

1. External surfaces of the console may be cleaned using a soft cloth and any ammonia-based window cleaner.
2. Be careful not to spill liquid cleaners into the printer, the disk drive, the microprocessor, or onto the keyboard.

Keyboard

1. Clean the surface of the keyboard and the keys with a paper towel lightly dampened with denatured alcohol.

2. If the keys become "sticky" or "jammed" causing characters to repeat across the screen, follow these steps:

   a. Turn power off.

   b. Run the heel of your hand across the keyboard: Do not use excessive force.

   c. Turn power on.

3. If keys still "stick" call your repairperson. He or she will have the necessary tools to remove particles from beneath the key caps.

4. Use a soft brush to dust in the spaces between the keys.

5. Do not put food, liquids or cigarette ashes near the keyboard; foreign particles may cause damage to the electronic components of the keyboard.

Printer

1. If you wish to clean the platen, remove it following the instructions in the printer section of your manual.

2. Lift off the platen, and clean it with a dry cloth or paper towel.

3. While the platen is removed, clean the inside of the printer by removing all paper and fibres, and clean the ink residue from the plastic card guide.

4. Wipe the carriage guide rails and other surfaces with a soft cloth moistened with a good grade household cleaner.

5. Do not spray cleaner directly into the printer.

6. Be sure to remove all cleaning implements from the printer after cleaning.

Printwheel

The printwheel will clog with ink and paper fibre over a period of time. Cleaning is indicated when printing quality decreases.

FIGURE 7-1
Proper cleaning prevents
problems

1. Remove the printwheel.
2. Dip a small type cleaning brush in liquid house-hold cleaner and brush the printwheel until it is clean.
3. Wipe dry with a clean lint-free cloth.
4. Replace the printwheel and secure the cover.

Caution: Never oil or lubricate the printer your-self. Your authorized service representative has the proper lubricant to ensure the best performance of your system.

Screen

1. Clean the glass CRT screen with any commer-cial, ammonia-based window cleaner.
2. If you are using a glare screen (see Chapter Nine for the section on filters) and it is smudged, re-move and clean it at the end of the day!
    - Rinse under cool water.
    - Towel dry.
    - Place the glare screen on a table, concave side up, to dry overnight.
3. If the glare screen is dusty, wipe it with a soft, dry, lint-free cloth.

Floppy Disks

Figure 7–2, Maxell's chart for Floppy Disk Handling and Storage, offers precautions to protect against pos-sible failure. In addition, there are many other obvi-ous ways to harm a floppy disk. Over a period of time the disk erodes. Users should stop using a floppy disk after it is two years old—provided that the floppy has been used with some consistency over that period.

FIGURE 7-2
Floppy disk handling and storage. *Courtesy: Maxell*

1. Do not touch disk surface. It is easily contaminated, which causes errors.

2. Do not use alcohol, thinners or freon to clean disk.

alcohol   thinner   freon

3. Do not use magnets or magnetized objects near the disk. Data can be lost from a disk exposed to a magnetic field.

4. Do not bend or fold the disk.

5. Do not place heavy objects on the disk.

6. Do not use rubber bands or paper clips on the disk.

7. Do not write on disk label with pencil or ball-point pen. Use felt-tip pen only.

label   index

pencil
pen

8. Do not use erasers on disk.

eraser

9. Apply index label to the right of Maxell label. Do not use labels in layers.

label   index

10. Insert carefully, by grasping upper edge and placing it into the drive.

disk drive

11. Keep disk in its protective envelope when not in use.

Floppy Disk

envelope

12. Disks not being used should be stored vertically in their box.

13. Do not expose the disk to excessive heat or sunlight.

14. Operating environment:
   A. Temperature: 10°C to 50°C (50°F to 122°F)
   B. Wet Bulb Temperature: Less than 29°C
   C. Relative Humidity: 20% to 80%

50° C
10° C
29° C under

15. Storage environment:
   A. Temperature: 4°C to 53°C (40°F to 127°F)
   B. Relative Humidity: 8% to 80%

53° C
4° C

16. While in transit the disk should be in its envelope in a protective box within the following ranges:
   A. Temperature: −40°C to 53°C (−40°F to 127°F)
   B. Relative Humidity: 8% to 90%

53° C
−40° C

The oxide coating on the floppy starts to shed at about age two. That shedding somehow brings on "reading" errors in the floppy serious enough at times to nullify all data on the disk. If the disk has been in a relatively low humidity environment, the oxide will start shedding well before the floppy is two years old. It is recommended that disks be stored in an environment with 40- to 60-percent humidity. You may consider using a hygrometer—a device to test relative humidity. Such devices cost about $25.

Diskette Fire Protection

Your business is as vulnerable as its records. And if your business records are kept on diskettes, your business is especially vulnerable. Diskettes can be destroyed in seconds. It does not take long for a fire to wipe out your vital records. At just 125° F, diskettes distort, and vital data are lost. Conventional insulated file cabinets may provide paper protection, but they cannot provide adequate protection for diskettes.

FIGURE 7-3
Diskette storage safe. *Courtesy: Victor Systems and Equipment*

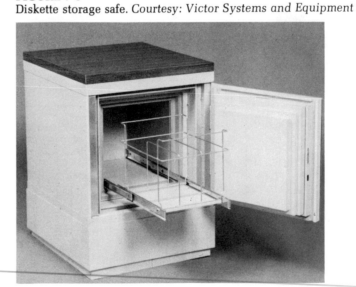

Diskette storage safes are designed for superior protection against the critical 125° heat level of diskette
distortion. See Figure 7–3. Delicate diskettes can be
damaged in other ways too. If the relative humidity
exceeds 85 percent, distortion kills the information
contained on diskettes. Dust and sunlight can also
ruin your information systems. And accidental
magnetic exposure erases information stored on diskettes. The records of your business can be destroyed
in seconds. And all you would have left would be
memories.

Shelf Life of Supplies

The date stamped on a box of cereal or a jar of mayon-
naise purchased in a supermarket gives a consumer
an indication of the recommended shelf life of the
product. Similarly, you should consider the shelf life
of your word processing supplies, especially when
you purchase in large quantities. Ribbons and some
floppy disks are no longer good after having sat in
your cabinet for six months without having been
used. The emulsions on top of the floppy disks tend
to oxidize—especially in a relatively moist atmo-
sphere—and then start to warp. The disk may also
lose its ability to hold magnetic impulses.

You can still purchase supplies in large quantities and enjoy the discount, but try to arrange with
the vendor to have a portion of the shipment delivered to you each month. That way you'll always have
fresh supplies. The dealer may not agree with the full
discount, but you may receive a price break that falls
somewhere between the high price for buying a dozen
disks and the low price for buying a gross outright.

Cleaning Your Own Diskette Heads

Closely related to the care and storage of your diskettes is the care of the recording heads on your diskette drive. This involves the internal workings of your

FIGURE 7-4
Head cleaning diskette kit (center). *Courtesy: 3M Corp.*

word processor, and ordinarily it would involve a call to a service technician. That service call, however, may not be necessary with a simple preventive maintenance practice. Special head-cleaning diskette kits let you clean the read-write heads on your 8-inch or 5¼-inch diskette drives. In just a few seconds, without any disassembly, mess, or bother, the heads can be completely cleansed of dirt, dust, magnetic oxides—all the things that can get into your machines every day.

The Data Recording Products Division of the 3M Corporation markets these kits. You simply saturate the special white cleaning pad in its jacket with the cleaning solution. Then insert the jacket into the diskette drive and turn it on. Your machine does the rest. The heads are microscopically cleaned without water or abrasion.

Static and Dust Problems

The people that operate your word processors may be building up a static charge. Just by taking a couple of steps across the floor in a well air-conditioned room, they can generate 5,000 volts or more. Or, in the wintertime 10,000 volts or more. Static can also be generated just by sitting down in a chair. And if the operator's next move is to touch one of your word processors, the result can be a blank screen, erratic data, spewing paper, or an altered memory. Static bombs can raise havoc with deadlines and increase workloads. Nothing could be more devastating than to have a complicated multipage document wiped out, and face the almost impossible task of trying to recreate it.

One solution to static, dust, and noise problems is the installation of high-performance, antistatic carpeting or static control floor mats. (See Figure 7–5.) Antistatic carpeting can limit static to well below the levels of sensitivity of word processors and computer terminals, and most electrostatically sensitive instrumentation. In addition to solving the static problem, the carpeting can eliminate dust conditions by gathering and holding particles until they can be removed. Without carpeting, the loose dust floats freely or is swirled into floppy disk drives with disastrous results.

Antistatic carpeting does not shed particles and cannot add to unclean conditions. Vacuuming the area every other day does away with possible dust problems. In addition to ending static and dust problems, the antistatic carpeting can reduce noise levels.

A less costly approach to static control is static control floor mats. Floor mats and runners create inexpensive islands and pathways of protection around and between sensitive areas. Static charges drain harmlessly from operators and other personnel as they walk, stand, or sit.

Another product that eliminates static problems is a liquid solution that sprays on your traditional carpet. Staticstop, manufactured by UTP, Inc., is a liquid spray that can be applied to your carpet, furniture, and other sources that might generate static.

Finally, if you store your floppy disks close to the floor—five feet or less—the cleaning personnel's vacuum cleaners or the maintenance crew's steel-wool floor polisher may very well wipe out information

FIGURE 7-5A
Static Stop antistatic spray.
Courtesy: UTP, Inc.

FIGURE 7-5B
Compu-Chair is an antistatic workstation chair. In combination with computer-grade static-controlled floor covering, Compu-Chair prevents static-caused equipment problems. *Courtesy: UTP, Inc.*

FIGURE 7-5C
Voltector Series 6 AC Power Conditioner is designed to protect terminals from powerline "noise" and from the destructive high-voltage surges that enter a building on the primary powerline. *Courtesy: Pilgrim Electric Co.*

FIGURE 7-5D
Static control floor mat. *Courtesy: 3M Corp.*

FIGURE 7-5E

stored on those floppies. How? The motors on both
the vacuum and the floor polisher set up magnetic
fields which, if close enough to the floppies, will play
tricks with the read/write surface. Moreover, small
pieces of steel wool from the polisher become airborne and at times scratch the diskettes. Worse yet: If
the equipment's cooling fan is running, it will pull
airborne pieces of steel into the system.[1]

Electric Power Surges

Electric power surges may enter your word processing area from your powerline and may damage your
word processing CPU. These uneven electrical power
surges may put your system out of service and require
extensive maintenance. Certain devices can prevent
harmful surges from reaching your valuable equipment by redirecting them to the ground. Two companies that specialize in this protection are Pilgrim
Electric Company and TII Industries, Inc. For more
information, you can write to:

Pilgrim Electric Co.		TII Industries, Inc.
29 Cain Drive		1375 Akron Street
Plainview, NY 11803	–or–	Copiague, NY 11726

Preventive Maintenance: Giving Your Printer Tender, Loving Care

When systems were changed from electromechanical
text editors to electronics, repairs to systems dramati-
cally decreased. Electronics and circuit board technology eliminated the maze of moving parts on most
screen-based systems. As a result, downtime was held
to a minimum.

The component of a word processor system,
however, that really "takes a workout" is the daisy

[1]*Inside Word Processing,* a publication of Buyers Laboratory, Inc.
Vol. 1, No. 5 (August, 1981), p. 4.

wheel printer. They often operate nonstop, from morning until night. And the component within the printer that takes the most abuse is the daisy wheel. This means frequent attention must be paid to the printwheel.

An intelligent, preventive maintenance program can prolong the life of your printer and printwheel and maintain letter-quality production.

Louis Kavanan, manager of printer supplies of Diablo Systems, suggests some guidelines for preventive maintenance for daisy wheel printers:

> One of the easiest methods of measuring print quality is to have on hand a comparative test—a master copy of a letter, for example—against which current samples are periodically compared. The operator looks for wear. After millions of impressions, the "lighter" weight parts of the font style, such as the serifs, the dot on the "i," the cross on the "t" may begin to degrade slightly. By maintaining a master copy, the very first signs of wear can be detected.[2]

Here are additional guidelines for the preventive maintenance of your daisy wheel printer.

1. Always check the operator's manual if you suspect any malfunction before calling a repairperson.

2. You can adjust the impact-energy setting to increase or lessen the impact of the printer. Too high a setting blurs the impression and wears the printwheels. Too low a setting generates light printing.

3. Use care when removing and replacing printwheels. Once the ribbon cartridge is removed and the hammer assembly tilted back, the daisy wheel should be lifted straight off by the cap—do not bend the petals. Hold the hammer assembly

[2]Kavanan, Louis, "Preventive Maintenance for Daisywheel Printers," *The Office* (June, 1982), p. 36.

back with one hand while doing this. Insert the new wheel making sure that it is aligned properly and seated firmly. Once it is placed on the hub, apply gentle finger pressure on the body of the wheel on either side of the cap to seat.

4. Store daisy wheels in a cool, dry area in a plastic case.

5. Make sure paper is inserted properly in the printer. If the paper is crumpled, it will jam the printer. Always place the top edge of the paper over the scale that rests on the platen. (See Figure 7–7.) This will insure that the paper does not roll up into the scale and become blocked as it advances upward.

FIGURE 7-6
Remove the print wheel by pulling upward on the print wheel knob. Pull gently but firmly. If the print wheel does not come free easily, push the print wheel knob from below. Never pull on the letter arms. Put all pressure on the solid knob.

FIGURE 7-7

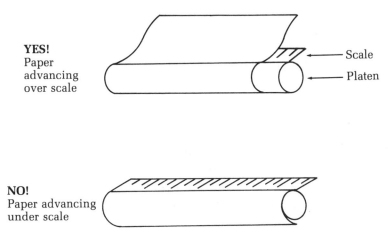

YES!
Paper advancing over scale

Scale
Platen

NO!
Paper advancing under scale

If for any reason the printer jams as a result of improper placement of paper, immediately stop the printer and remove the crumpled paper by pulling the paper release lever forward and removing the paper and/or remnants.

A staple is another way to damage the printer. Never insert paper into your printer that contains a staple. The character on the daisy wheel can be damaged if it strikes the staple.   **133**

Don't Try to Fix Everything on Your Printer

If your printer prints "garbage," turn the printer off and turn it on again. It may be a bad contact that has to be reset. If, on the other hand, you come across a problem that you cannot fix, do not attempt to take apart the printer to find the cause. Call the service repairperson. Common sense should prevail. Some repairs should be serviced only by an authorized representative.

WORD PROCESSING SECURITY

Word processors, small computers, telephones, and other office equipment have been big items on a growing number of thieves' shopping lists. In fact, more than $94,000,000 worth of office equipment was stolen in 1980, according to the Uniform Crime Reports Section of the Federal Bureau of Investigation.

An effective way to hold on to your word processor is to secure it to your desk with a special adhesive pad. Unlike the usual bolt-down devices, the pads lock office machines to furniture without marring it. They can be removed by a heat process. Prices range from $60 for an Anchor Dot, which handles telephones, dictation equipment and small instruments, up to $440 for security racks, which fasten separate components of computer systems together. Information on these protective pads can be obtained by writing to Anchor Pad International, Inc., in Marina Del Rey, California.

FIGURE 7-8
Power lock switch

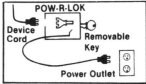

SERVICE

It has been well documented that one of the primary considerations in selecting word processing equipment is reliability. In other words, rapid servicing outranks other considerations for managers who find long downtime disastrous. Information managers who are responsible for word processing operations know that a day's downtime, or more, can mean a big backlog in terms of processing vital information.

Turnaround time on downtime service of the system is critical. And the questions that managers and word processor owners often ask is "How soon can you get a part replaced, and how long will it take to have me 'up and running'?"

Guidelines for a Good Servicing Policy

1. *Track Record of the Vendor.* A strong commitment to good service throughout the industry. An earned reputation by users, consultants, and industry publications is a good yardstick to measure reliability.

2. *Qualified Technicians.* Extensive training in electronic skills and technology for customer service representatives. A good indication of a well qualified technician is the intensity and quality of instruction each candidate must go through to learn about the vendor's products and peripherals.

3. *Keeping Abreast of Technology by Technicians.* A good indication of quality service results from companies that continually upgrade technicians' skills and knowledge. As technicians complete more courses, they receive more responsibility and recognition by the vendor. A vendor who has a policy of rewarding outstanding performance by technicians, will result in more productive and efficient service for you, the word processor user.

4. *To Be There When You Need Them.* How can you be sure the vendor will be there whenever you need service? Ask for a guarantee. This should be "spelled out" in a yearly service contract. This contract should include unlimited service calls.

5. *Turnaround Time.* The technician should be there, in most cases, within four hours. In addition, the technician should regularly perform preventive maintenance inspections—whether or not you need service—just to prevent problems.

Vendors should be able to repair your systems quickly on the premises. The technician should be able to run a diagnostic test on your equipment, using special equipment, and/or a special test disk. A diagnostic test quickly isolates any problems to one circuit board. After replacing the defective board, the technician can take it back to a local service center for repair.

Some vendors have initiated a service dispatching system to improve customer service. The customer calls a Customer Service Center which is tied into a computerized system that alerts an appropriate technician. This new system is a way to cut the response time to service calls.

6. *Service Cost.* Service cost should be moderate since many word processing systems contain circuit boards that can be repaired locally. Vendors usually do not have to maintain such a large circuit board inventory. This reduces operating costs and, therefore, vendors should be able to pass those savings on to you.

7. *Service Network.* Is the vendor's service network large enough to handle a multilocation company? An established vendor usually can handle most locations throughout the country. Look for a vendor that has a service office in your area.

With the introduction of many lower-priced word processor "writer" systems, vendors have reduced or eliminated "after-sale" support. A recent study,[3] however, finds that major industry suppliers are risking the loss of large shares by decreasing support services to end users. This study means that users must be supported after the sale to ensure the system works for them. And, in spite of the trend of lower-cost systems and reduced services, users are going to seek out those vendors that provide adequate support, service, and training.

Operational Problems (Marketing Support)

At times a word processor user has an application problem that is unrelated to a hardware malfunction. He or she simply needs an answer to a procedural step

[3]"User Feedback: The Impact of Support on Vendor Selection," The Sierra Group, P.O. Box 26212, Tempe, AZ 85284.

and is unable to locate the solution in the vendor's manual. To solve this problem, vendors have installed a "hot-line" number that users can call and obtain immediate answers.

Mixed Vendor Support

There can be a real service problem with vendor support when the system consists of more than one vendor's product. The owner who mixes components from different vendors may pay a price for so doing. If your system goes down, the serviceperson from Vendor No. 1 will say, "Of course you're going down all the time—it's a feature of Vendor No. 2's printer." When you call Vendor No. 2, the serviceperson may tell you, "Didn't you know that Vendor No. 1's disk drives are known for their high failure rate?"

Built-In Back-Up Systems

Many advanced word processing systems are striving to set a new standard for environmental tolerance and reliability. They are designed to be highly tolerant of static discharges that are common in dry climates and heated offices.

An optional built-in battery, plus a highly sophisticated power supply that prevents loss of your office information, is available (on some systems) if a brown-out or power failure should occur.

A Way to Keep Your System "Always Up"

You can investigate service contracts and negotiate an agreement with your vendor to provide a replacement for your WP system in case there is an extended breakdown. This is a way to insure that your office work does not stop if your system has to be taken to the shop.

Some systems go beyond this by providing a

built-in back-up into the system. This means that each unit contains its own built-in duplicate to keep you going if a failure should occur and to protect your information from loss or damage due to mechanical or electrical problems. When information goes in, it is stored in both sides. Each side is independent of its duplicate. At all times, each side of this fully redundant system is checking on the well-being of the other side. If one should detect a malfunction in any part of the other, it automatically shuts down that side and takes over all functions. Your office work goes on without disruption.

Built-In Back-Ups
with Electronic Service Call Tie-In

Meanwhile the "up" (running) side automatically dials a toll-free 800 vendor service phone number. Your vendor service department runs remote diagnostics on the "down" side and contacts the local WP vendor service office. This is all done without anyone in your office having to know that anything was wrong until the WP serviceperson phones to arrange a convenient time for a service call.

The *failure protection techniques* used in this method were developed for the space program by NASA. Recent cost reductions in electronic technology have made their application to office equipment economically practical. Many WP vendors have taken the lead in applying this advanced technology. Companies that design, manufacture, and sell WP equipment are beginning to realize the importance of good maintenance and support *after the sale is made!* They are taking the time to understand the needs of offices and then building office automation products to meet those needs. Progressive manufacturers of WP systems are taking a more careful look at the "human side" and are using technology to solve these "human office problems."

Supplies and Accessories 8

Once you have purchased your word processor, the cash outlay does not end. The expense of supplies and accessories can be a substantial part of your budget. Up to this point, our discussion has focused on the word processor itself. This chapter will explore a not-so-glamorous, but extremely important aspect of the word processing system. This is the area of the supplies that fuel your word processors, as well as the accessories that integrate your word processor with other office technologies. You can appreciate the value of supplies if you suddenly find yourself out of ribbons or continuous forms in the middle of an important run. Lack of a $12 printwheel can stop a $12,000 word processor dead in its tracks and idle a $250-a-week employee.

WP SUPPLIES AND THE GROWING CONSUMABLE RATE

Depending upon your applications and on the volume of work generated, your word processor usually has a healthy appetite for supplies. Ribbons, diskettes, printwheels, and forms make up the common supplies. Even a small word processor, for example, can eat nearly half its original cost in ribbons, diskettes, and printwheels in the course of a year.

Matching Supplies to Hardware Technology

As new hardware technology is introduced, manufacturers of supplies and accessories are constantly trying to keep up with, and even anticipate, equipment trends. There is a large and growing "office automation aftermarket." Manufacturers of supplies generally follow, and they are dependent on the hardware systems market, developing their products to match the hardware needs of users.

Correction fluid, for instance, is a product that depends on the typewriter, an early form of office automation. Were it not for the typewriter, there would be no need for correction fluid. As screen-based systems proliferate, the need diminishes for correction supplies, such as the eraser, correction fluid, and carbon paper. The life cycle of high technology supplies is much shorter than those of conventional office supplies. Many of the new products are technically obsolete by the time they are on the market because of the speed of technological advancement. For automation supplies manufacturers, the trick is to keep pace with the technology, constantly revising or changing products to keep up with the needs.

WP Suppliers: Who Are They?

Will the real suppliers please stand up? Word processing suppliers are a mixed assortment of brand name manufacturers and "private label" distributors all vying for a share of this booming market. "Big league" brand name suppliers are plentiful. Manufacturers may also subcontract private-label products from a "secondary manufacturer," who, in turn, may have "private-labeled" the goods itself. In this kind of environment, claims of product superiority are devious.

There are currently two trends in the marketplace: first, declining equipment costs (and with them, a growing automation market among smaller users), and second, rising selling costs. As the machines become smaller and less expensive, reaching the potential customer becomes a much bigger problem.

Because it is costly to sell to small users scattered around a geographical area, there is a shift away from manufacturer-direct selling. The effect has been to move responsibility for supply selection and vendor assignment to the end user. In one sense, the user has gained from a wider choice of products and outlets— and at the same time, the problem of making a selection becomes a little more bewildering.

TABLE 8-1

Purchasing Magnetic Media: Analyzing Distribution Channels.

	ORIGINAL EQUIPMENT MANUFACTURERS (OEM)	MEDIA MANUFACTURERS	OFFICE SUPPLY DEALER	MAIL ORDER	COMPUTER STORE	DIRECT SALES
ADVANTAGES	• Insures use of proper media, especially if special formats are necessary. • Warranty agreements imply media is covered with equipment.	• Support and toll-free (800) numbers available. • Warranties on media. • Brand recognition.	• Convenience of purchase. (Any media with other office supplies). • Immediate delivery. • Offers variety of product offering. • Local source.	• Largest product offering. • Easy ordering procedures. • Low prices and user quantity discounts. • Depending on quantity purchased, an average of 25 percent off list price can be saved.	• Purchases can be made from seller of equipment. • Insures proper media selection. • Immediate delivery. • Local source.	• Varied product offering. • Direct contact with seller provides support to user.
DISADVANTAGES	• Lack of support for media sales due to its small percentage of corporate sales. • Long wait for product delivery (4-8 weeks). • High selling price.	• Usually sell through distributors and dealers, unless very large end user. • Quantity discounts often unavailable to end user.	• Lack of expertise in sale of media.	• Can't see product prior to purchase (sometimes results in delivery of a substitute item).	• Salespersons' knowledge of media often limited to only those products compatible with the systems they sell.	• Usually does not stock inventory, therefore, this causes delivery delays.

Source: Dennison/National Co. Holyoke, MA

There are at least six purchasing avenues open to users of magnetic media. Criteria of quality, service, and support should be weighed equally with price. Table 8–1 suggests some of the purchasing avenues for word processor owners looking to purchase magnetic media.

Matching Equipment with Supply Brand Names

There are two schools of thought and some users are content to purchase off-brand name supplies if they are less expensive than brand names. Others rely on the prestige (and in some cases on the superior quality) of brand names. They reason that printwheels and ribbon cartridges are as much a part of the total WP system as the printer or terminal, and both of these supplies have an effect on the output of the system. In sticking with a brand name that matches your piece of equipment, you rely on the manufacturer taking into account meticulous design factors within the system. Weight and dimensional tolerance on printwheels are critical, for instance, and have a pronounced effect on printer life and output quality. Off-brand ribbons that do not match the equipment may lead to degraded output, jamming and ribbon spoilage. Of course, economics is the prime factor for choosing off-brand WP supplies. Brand-name supplies are usually more expensive.

Guidelines for Selecting Office Automation Supplies

What should you look for when you're choosing an office automation supplier? The National Office Products Association offers the following guidelines:[1]

---

[1]Mueller, Robert, "Feeding the Automated Office," *Information & Records Management* (February, 1982), p. 23.

Experience—Does the supplier have enough experience to be able to give sound product advice, as well as advice on office procedures? Can the vendor keep you current on new ideas, products, and techniques for improving office productivity?

Sophistication—Is the supplier keeping up with new technologies and systems? Is training and guidance in automation supplies use offered?

Trained Personnel—Are the supplier's employees experienced enough to provide sound product advice and proper selection for your needs?

Service—Does the supplier take time to get to know you and your needs? Does she or he volunteer ideas to help you cut costs and improve productivity?

Stability—Is the supplier financially sound? Can you depend on an on-going source of supply?

Inventory Breadth—Does the supplier stock the products you need in sufficient depth to fill your ordinary requirements quickly? Is there easy access to a wholesaler or manufacturer warehouse which can ship products quickly?

Flexibility—Can the supplier meet unusual demands when required to do so?

Value—Does the supplier offer good value for the prices charged?

Location—Can the supplier deliver quickly and respond to service calls in a timely manner?

Some independent suppliers, such as Inmac of Santa Clara, California (see Appendix), offer products that have a no-risk double-protection guarantee. Any product in their catalog may be returned within 45 days, and they offer a one-year replacement guarantee.

PRINTWHEELS

There are two varieties of printwheels—plastic and metal. Plastic printwheels offer good print quality and economy. Metal printwheels, by virtue of their metal coatings, are extremely tough, and they offer a very high quality print image, especially when used with a multistrike ribbon. Both types offer 10-pitch and 12-pitch wheels.

Obviously, a printwheel isn't worth its character set without a ribbon to carry the image to the printed surface. There are three basic ribbon types.

Fabric ribbons are made of cloth that is looped and loaded into the cartridge to put a continuous cycle of ribbon in front of the printwheel. As it is used, the ribbon gradually loses its density, signaling the user that it is time to change the cartridge. And when it is time to change the cartridge, there is no direct contact with the ribbon itself. Fabric ribbons offer both quality and economy.

Multistrike ribbons come wound reel-to-reel in a cartridge. They are also easy to load and eliminate all direct contact with the ribbon. Multistrike ribbons produce a quality print image, and with new high-capacity black multistrike cartridges, they also offer tremendous savings in cost per character.

The *single strike ribbon,* like the multistrike ribbon, comes wound reel-to-reel in a cartridge. Single strike ribbons, however, create the highest quality impression. They're best used when the requirement is for reproduction quality.

Changing Your
Printwheel for a Variety of Applications

You can expand the usefulness of your word processor by employing a variety of printwheels for different applications. You can have your corporate logo, scientific symbols, ideograms—just about anything that is reproducible—inserted into a metal or plastic printwheel in place of an unwanted character.

Applications

1. Instead of repeating a long corporate name in your sales letters, presentations, or proposals, your logo can be typed right into the text.

FIGURE 8-1
Dramco's Stock Characters. *Courtesy: Dramco Sales, Inc.*

DRAMCO'S STOCK CHARACTERS

MISCELLANEOUS
- @ commercial "at"
- # number
- % percent
- ® registry
- © copyright
- TM trademark
- ○ circle
- □ square
- ◊ diamond
- ♁ beaker
- / slash
- ♀ female
- ♂ male
- ⧧ group mark
- ‡ record mark
- ⧻ segment mark
- ⌑ lozenge
- ꝗ substitute
- ~ logical not
- ≡ identical with
- \ reverse slant
- ‰ percent

FRACTIONS
- ½ one half
- ¼ one quarter
- ¾ three quarters
- ⅜ three eighths
- ⅝ five eighths
- ½ one half
- ¼ one quarter
- ¾ three quarters
- ½" one half inch
- ¾" three quarter inch
- 5/4" five quarters inch
- 1" one inch
- ⅞ seven eighths
- ⅛ one eighth
- ⅓ one third
- ⅜ three eighths
- ⅛ one eighth
- ⅝ five eighths
- ⅞ seven eighths
- 5/4 five fourths

CURRENCY
- $ dollar (U.S.)
- £ pound sterling
- ¥ yen
- $ dollar
- £ pound sterling
- DM german mark
- ₱ pence

TYPOGRAPHICAL
- . period
- , comma
- : colon
- ; semi-colon
- - dash
- _ underscore
- ‗ double underscore
- ? question mark
- ! exclamation mark
- (left parenthesis
-) right parenthesis
- [left bracket
-] right bracket
- † dagger
- ‡ double dagger
- § section
- ¶ paragraph
- ' apostrophe
- " quotation
- & ampersand
- & ampersand
- ★ asterisk
- ~ tilde
- ⌢ circumflex
- ¯ macron
- ˘ breve
- ¨ diaresis
- ¸ cedilla
- ´ acute
- ` grave
- | vertical line

LANGUAGE
- ¡ inverted exclamation
- ¿ inverted question
- Ñ n ya
- Æ ligature UC
- æ ligature lc
- Å angstrom
- Ä umlaut A (UC)
- Ö umlaut O (UC)
- Ü umlaut U (UC)
- ä umlaut a (l.c.)
- ö umlaut o (l.c.)
- ü umlaut u (l.c.)
- ñ n ya
- Œ diphthong UC
- œ diphthong lc
- á a accent acute
- à a accent grave
- é e accent acute
- è e accent grave
- ê e accent circumflex
- ç c cedilla

MATHEMATICAL
- + plus
- − minus
- ± plus/minus
- ∓ minus/plus
- √ radical
- ∫ integral
- ÷ divided
- × times
- · times dot
- = equal
- ≠ not equal
- ~ similar
- ≈ approx. equal
- ≡ identical
- < less than
- > greater than
- ≤ less than or equal
- ≥ greater than or equal
- ≦ less than or equal
- ≧ greater than or equal
- ∞ infinity
- ′ prime
- ″ double prime
- ∩ logical product
- ∪ logical sum
- ⊂ contained in
- ⊃ excluded from
- ∈ exists
- { brackets
- } brackets
- ⟨ brackets
- ⟩ brackets

TECHNICAL
- ↑ arrow up
- ↓ arrow down
- ← arrow left
- → arrow right
- Ω ohm
- μ mu
- ∇ inverted delta
- Ø cancelled zero
- 0 9 8 7 6 5 4 3 2 1 subscripts
- 0 9 8 7 6 5 4 3 2 1 exponents
- ℃ Celsius
- mm millimeter
- cm centimeter
- km kilometer
- m/m millimeter
- mm² square millimeter
- m/m² square millimeter
- cm² square centimeter
- ● burger dot
- ° degrees

continued
- cm³ cubic centimeter
- m² square meter
- m³ cubic meter
- △ triangle
- ⅄ 32/49
- μV millivolt
- μF milliFaraday
- ∡ angle
- ∢ angle
- ∿ (32/42)
- cyl cylinder
- sph sphere

GREEK ALPHABET
- α alpha (lc)
- β beta (lc)
- γ gamma (lc)
- δ delta (lc)
- ε epsilon (lc)
- ζ zeta (lc)
- η eta (lc)
- θ theta (lc)
- ι iota (lc)
- κ kappa (lc)
- λ lambda (lc)
- μ mu (lc)
- ν nu (lc)
- ξ xi (lc)
- π pi (lc)
- ρ rho (lc)
- σ sigma (lc)
- τ tau (lc)
- φ phi (lc)
- χ chi (lc)
- ψ psi (lc)
- ω omega (lc)
- Γ Gamma (UC)
- Δ Delta (UC)
- Θ Theta (UC)
- Λ Lambda (UC)
- Ξ Xi (UC)
- Π Pi (UC)
- Σ Sigma (UC)
- Φ Phi (UC)
- Ψ Psi (UC)
- Ω Omega (UC)

2. Instead of writing in the symbol for frequently used foreign currency, you can type it in. Foreign language symbols, such as the inverted Spanish question mark, can be typewritten.

3. Engineering and electronic symbols can be typed into your specifications, manuals, and purchase orders. Mathematical equations that formerly had to be handwritten (see Chapter Five) can be typed effortlessly and with perfect clarity.

STORAGE DISKS

As mentioned in Chapter One, floppy disks are the primary storage medium for most word processors. They range from the 5¼- to 8-inch size and stored from 143,000 to 250,000 bytes of memory respectively. A new family of 3½-inch "micro-floppy" disk drives is now available. These micro disks store exactly the same as the 5¼-inch disks.

Characteristically, the Winchester disks are not removable and are built into the systems. They have a larger storage capacity (up to 10,000,000 bytes) and are complementary to floppy disks.

Optical disks are becoming viable contenders for Winchester disk drives. The key attraction of optical disk storage technologies centers upon the high stor-

FIGURE 8-2
A new Hewlett-Packard family of 3½-inch "micro-floppy" disk drives is now available. The shirt-pocket-sized 3½-inch disk (at the right) is compared with 8-inch and 5¼-inch flexible disks. *Courtesy: Hewlett-Packard*

FIGURE 8-3A
Winchester disk drive model 4000 vertical. *Courtesy: Shugart Associates*

age capacity and compactness. Optical disk storage is massive. We no longer talk in terms of mega (million) bytes when we measure storage for opticals. Our unit of measurement is gigabytes (billion). A 12-inch optical disk can store two gigabytes of data—or the entire contents of the *Encyclopedia Britannica* on a single side.

Laser video disk products should provide 10 to 20 gigabits (10 to 20 billion bits) of usable information per disk. Initial laser video disk units will offer permanent recording only on each disk and thus will be used primarily for archival files (like microfiche). As video disk technology provides cost-effective renewable disks, similar to current magnetic disk usage, 147

FIGURE 8-3B
The MnemoDisc℠ is comparable to a long-playing record in both size and cost. The 12-inch plastic disk is produced by a process that employs electronic beam and laser technologies to store over 6,000 pages of images. Each image is reduced 88 times and laid out in the disk in concentric rings. *Courtesy: Mnemos, Inc.*

they will find use as working file storage, among other things.[2]

A new information storage and retrieval system utilizing electronic beam, laser and electronic technologies allows the user to store over 6,000 pages of letter-sized documents on a single 12-inch plastic MnemeDisc℠.

Filing Floppy Disks

Diskettes can be filed in a cost-effective system for efficient organization, indexing, and retrieval by using your own standard filing cabinets. Filing disks in this matter will not ensure them against loss of fire (see Chapter Seven, Figure 7–3), but they are expedient for temporary and noncritical information. The easy-to-attach special file bar converts any pocket protector or sleeve for convenient filing in standard file cabinets, desklike file drawers, or revolving carrousels. Figure 8–4 illustrates disks inserted into

[2]Blackmarr, Brian, "Office 2000," *Words*, June–July, 1982, p. 17.

FIGURE 8-4
Inexpensive correspondence files from Dennison National Company come with copper-reinforced binder holes. *Courtesy: Dennison/National Co.*

copper-reinforced binder holders. National's file bar can be attached to this or to any other three-hole punched sheet, so they can be used in a standard file cabinet.

Identifying Diskettes

With the growth of floppy diskettes as the standard storage medium for word processors, there is a need to identify each diskette. Self-adhesive word processing labels specially designed for diskettes lets the user see what information is stored on each disk without having to put them into the machine. Because they provide a large, easy-to-read space, you can list what you have recorded on the disks. The self-adhesive labels are removable and come in sizes to fit both floppy disks and mini-floppy disks. When all the necessary information is written on the label, it should be placed on the disk, rather than on the envelope. The information should be written on the label before it is attached so that the pen strokes will not damage the disk.

FIGURE 8-5
Pocket protector sleeves for filing diskettes and hard paper copy together. *Courtesy: Dennison/National Co.*

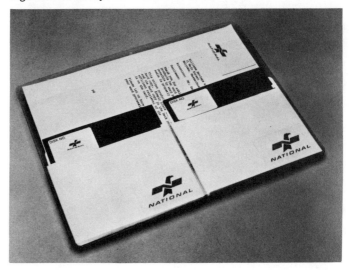

FIGURE 8-6
Self-adhesive labels for disks. *Courtesy: Avery Label*

If you have mailing lists to print, the new word processing address labels have been designed to work with most word processing printers.

Automatic Envelope Feeder

An automatic envelope feeder attaches to the printer. Envelope feeders hold over 200 envelopes at a time (sizes 6 and 10). The device automatically feeds envelopes into the printer aligning the typing position at a rate of up to three envelopes every 10 seconds.

Automatic Sheet Feeder

A combination automatic dual-sheet and envelope feeder is available for attachment to printers. New technology in dual-sheet and envelope feeders allows the automatic feeding of cut sheets of paper from either of two paper trays, and envelopes from an envelope tray directly into a printer under control of sig-

FIGURE 8-7
The Ziyad Z-3000 paper processor. *Courtesy: Ziyad, Inc.*

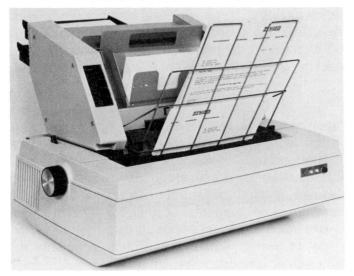

nals stored as part of the text or menu. Printed sheets and envelopes are automatically ejected from the printer and collated in correct printing sequence in the output basket. A feed slot is available for operator manual insertion of nonstandard sheets of envelopes without having to remove the dual sheet and envelope feeder from the printer. The new dual sheet and envelope feeder was designed by Zilyad, Inc., and is pictured in Figure 8–8.

TRACTORS

Tractors are used with continuous form paper. They are fitted on a printer and the forms tractor guides the paper through the printer. Forms tractors work on a sprocket method. The teeth of the tractor fit into the perforated holes which run along the sides of the continuous forms. As the sprockets on the tractor turn, the paper is pulled through the printer, holding it in stable position. Continuous-form stationery is not as attractive as single sheets and may not be acceptable for sending letters to customers and clients. It is used for rough-draft copies and business forms such as purchase orders and/or receipts.

BURSTERS

Bursters separate the continuous form paper into single sheets after it has passed through the printer. This device is called a forms burster and automatically processes the continuous forms by cutting and stacking them into single sheet piles for further use.

SHREDDERS

Paper shredders are a protection against security breach. They are devices that destroy large amounts of high security documents into minute shreds. Shredders are used with single documents feed, but also can be used for lengthy continuous forms. As more and more companies become involved in sensitive research in product development, shredders offer a way to protect sensitive confidential documents from falling into unauthorized hands.

Sometimes a paper shredder is not enough. It does not destroy all the confidential material. There are stories of people piecing together shredded documents. According to newspaper accounts, investigators sorted the shredded material by looking at the color, length, texture, and weight of the paper, and at the typefaces and weight of the printing. They were able to reunite letters and other security documents. This would have been impossible had the material been destroyed by a security disintegrator. With a disintegrator, the paper is cut so fine, there's simply no way to reconstruct original documents. The rotating bias-cut knives repeatedly slice the material to be destroyed until it becomes confetti that will fall through a screen. Figures 8–8 and 8–9 illustrate security disintegrators.

DISINTEGRATORS

FIGURE 8-8
Disintegrator. *Courtesy: Security Engineered Machinery*

OTHER WORKSTATION ACCESSORIES

Wrist Support Platform

We have learned in our typewriting class to keep wrists straight and elbows at 90° when we keyboard on traditional electric typewriters. But if keyboards are elevated more than 1¼" at the front—as is the case of many detached keyboards—tension can develop. A special wrist support, which is a little platform that slips under keyboards to provide a slanted deck extension to support palms, helps to relieve wrist stress. The accessory is designed to provide support with a barely perceptible springiness that responds to the

FIGURE 8-10
Exxon 520 information processor has extended keyboard for palm rest. *Courtesy: Exxon Office Systems*

FIGURE 8-11
Wrist support cuts stress

weight of hands and makes the support adaptable to most keyboards 1¼″ high or more. (See Figure 8–11.) In addition, some word processors have extended keyboards for palm rests. (See Figure 8–10.)

Footrest

To elevate your feet and overcome any potential ache that might creep into your lower back and put your legs to sleep, you can use a metal footrest. This accessory is 14″ wide × 12″ deep; 5″ high at back, 3″ high at

FIGURE 8-12
Footrest fights fatigue

front. By scooting footrest forward and backward, you can compensate for your height in relation to working surface height. This is ideal for word processing operators or anyone who's desk-bound. (See Figure 8–12.)

Ergonomics 9

The most successful examples of offices to have implemented automation have looked not only at the mechanics of the hardware and software, at the emotional and psychological impact on people, but also at the physical design of the workstation as it fits into the total office environment. Since employees spend more time at the place of work than in any other one place, it behooves management to provide an environment that is both pleasant and healthful. The whole area of physical design is called *ergonomics*. Ergonomics is the study of the interface of man and machine, as well as how to achieve the delicate balance that will provide an environment conducive to productive and satisfying work.

The heart of any office is people. As more and more people spend more and more time at word processors and computer terminals, it is important that the workplace become humanized. Word processors must be easy to use, and comfortable to work with. As workers realize that the new devices are to be **157**

FIGURE 9-1
The word processing environment. *Courtesy: Honeywell*

staples in the work diet for years to come, smart vendors and designers of systems must pay attention to the human side of the equation. Vendors cannot think all they have to do is turn out a good machine, and walk away from the human element.

PHYSICAL ATTRIBUTES OF A GOOD WORD PROCESSOR

A good word processor must possess those attributes that make it comfortable and easy to use. It means that the end user should have the benefits of human-engineered display terminals. It means the keyboard is detached, the display tiltable, and the range of phosphors easy on the eyes.

Once you start using a word processor, you will find it takes some getting used to, even if you already have conventional typing skills. The word processor—with a screen—is another kind of machine, and most office or home environments are poorly equipped to deal with it. While organizations these days go to a lot of trouble in planning word processing areas correctly, they are not usually so fussy about such things as lighting and terminal positions on workers' desks. After all, they reason, you as an operator will not be sitting in front of the screen for eight hours every day. But operators may experience discomfort, headaches, eyestrain, or neck stiffness. The developing science of ergonomics is beginning to address these problems, and systems designers are beginning to set the stage for a more comfortable environment.

One of the best examples of an ergonomically sound word processor is the Micom 3003 by Philips Information Systems. This system includes many of the features that contribute to operator comfort and productivity and that has consistently ranked at the top of user surveys for ease of use and performance.

Complete Viewing Comfort

Screens should be clear with sharp characters to accommodate your applications without straining eyes—even after hours of operation. High-quality *dot-matrix* design produces upper- and lower-case text featuring true character descenders, without flicker or distortion, to give you optimum readability and freedom from eye fatigue.

Glare-Resistant Screen

Eyestrain, according to the National Institute for Occupational Safety and Health, is a problem affecting over 80 percent of all VDT operators. When operators don't strain their eyes, they become more alert. This helps to reduce careless errors and helps increase productivity.

There are solutions. Tinted glass, for instance, will help reduce glare. An etched screen surface that minimizes glare from office and window light is another. An etched screen reduces sharpness but

FIGURE 9-2

Polaroid's CP-70 contrast enhancement filter absorbs the harsh reflections and ambient reflected glare, which contribute to eye strain and fatigue for operators of video display terminals (VDTs). The filter incorporates a circular polarizer, which improves the contrast of VDT screen displays while eliminating reflections of lights, people and objects in the surrounding environment. To attach the filter, self-adhesive Velcro strips stick to the bezel around the VDT screen. *Courtesy: Polaroid*

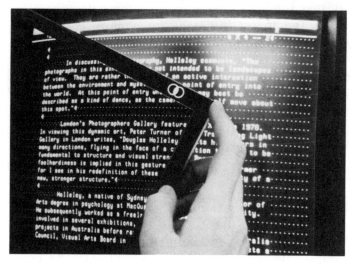

FIGURE 9-3

Polaroid circular polarizers act as a light trap. Ambient light can go through the polarizer, but light reflected from the tube face can't get out. The result is contrast enhancement of the display. *Courtesy: Polaroid*

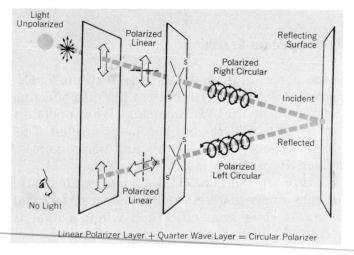

usually will not improve contrast. A better alternative would be to use filters that fit over your screen. Word processor users can now purchase separate filters (see Figure 9–2) that fit directly over the screen. One manufacturer, Polaroid, distributes the Polaroid CP-70 Contrast Enhancement Filter for video display terminals. It enhances contrast and reduces glare.

Rearranging lighting, walls, and windows can also reduce glare. Avoid placing your screen so that you face a window or sit with your back to it. Both positions add glare to the screen and induce fatigue and eyestrain. Position your screen so that you sit at right angles to the window, and lower the blinds.

Harsh overhead lighting should be avoided, if possible. You can install grid diffusers over the ceiling lights or you can arrange special *task-ambient lighting* that provides light directly at your work area. If you need extra light, you can get a draftsman's lamp with a flexible head that can be turned away from the screen, and directed onto the papers you are working with. (See Figure 9–4.)

FIGURE 9-4

Another solution to glare would be to attach a hood to the terminal screen. However, you must be careful not to cover the vents in the terminal housing with homemade devices. The heat inside will not dissipate if there is anything covering them, and it can become intense if the vents are covered for any length of time.

Screen Height and Angle Adjustment

Provisions for operator adjustment for screen height and angle to meet eye level should be available. This will further reduce glare.

FIGURE 9-5

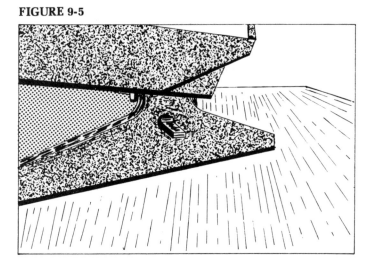

Brightness and Contrast Controls

An operator-adjustable intensity wheel (or knob) should be available to lighten or darken screen characters to suit individual preferences, while its contrast wheel (or knob) highlights input fields and dims formats to clearly guide your operators through keyboarding.

System Status (Format) Line

Your word processor should contain a protected status line or format line to give you the comfort of always knowing, at a glance, your present format, spacing, margins, tab settings—your complete system activity and availability.

Light, Compact Design

The cabinet design should be small enough to leave you plenty of work space. It should be lightweight to permit easy transfer to another office or desk by any member of your staff. Some systems occupy less desk space than an open looseleaf binder.

Do You Wear Glasses?

If you wear glasses you might have to make some adjustments. The screen distance is somewhat greater than comfortable reading distance, so you may consider obtaining a special pair of glasses to compensate for the change of distance. Special bifocals are designed to combine lenses for screen and reading distances. Your ophthalmologist may advise tinting the glasses slightly to reduce glare.

Seating Position and Distance

The diagram in Figure 9–6 shows the human body seated at a visual display terminal with lines drawn to indicate the angles of vision and posture, with relative relationships between the human and the machine.

KEYBOARDING CONVENIENCE

Word processing keyboards should emulate the standard keyboards of office typewriters that operators are accustomed to using. This familiar layout will ensure operator confidence when learning your system. The

FIGURE 9-6
Ergoeuropa. *Courtesy: Wang Laboratories*

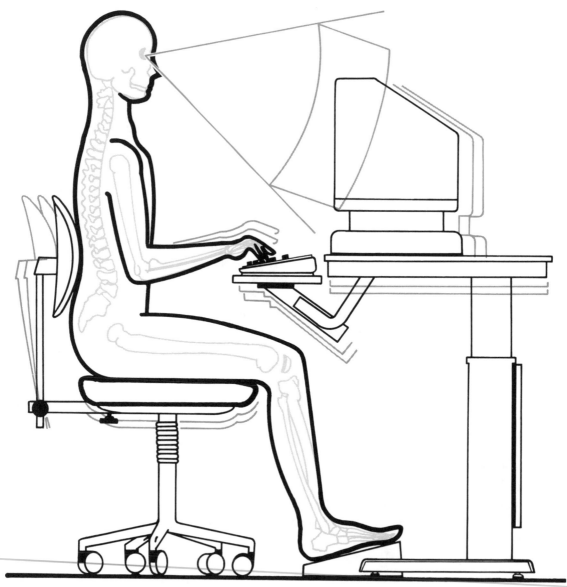

FIGURE 9-7

Philips 3004, a "human engineered" standalone word processing system that combines word and data processing capabilities. *Courtesy Philips Information System*

following guidelines should also be considered in total keyboarding convenience:

Operator-Adjustable—Keyboards should be separated from the display (cable connected) for independent operation up to two feet away, so your operators may place them in the most convenient position. (See Figure 9–8.)

Adjustable Keyboarding "Clicks"—Most systems have built-in speakers with volume control to allow operators an adjustable audible "click" option when keyboarding.

Sculptured keytops—Keytops are individually sculptured to allow fingertips to strike each key squarely, so you make fewer mistakes. Each key's pressure-response action and "click" provides positive input. A large palm rest should be integrated just below the keys. And all keys should be clearly labeled and color-coded to eliminate confusion when keying multiple functions.

165

FIGURE 9-8
Xerox 820 information processor. Separate keyboard provides flexibility for operator. *Courtesy: Xerox Corp.*

Minimum Function Keys—There should be a minimum function key for keyboarding simplicity. Single keys such as a single Clear key that erases the entire screen is preferable to having to code several keys for a single function.

Repeat Keys—Frequently used keys such as hyphens and dashes should repeat when held down to save keystrokes.

Some personal computers have "membrane keyboards," which are flat keyboards built into the surface. Their main advantages are lower cost and resistance to spills and to other forms of contamination. Touch typists have trouble with them since the typists are used to being able to depress keys farther than the switches on a membrane keyboard move. It can also be hard to tell where one key ends

166 and another begins.

Modular Components

Manufacturers of furniture and furnishings offer a wide array of modular workstations and compqnents to meet the requirements of the electronic office. Available in both keyboard and desk heights, communication station furniture accommodates most word processing systems and peripherals. Special workstation furniture addresses the need for a satisfying work environment providing safety, comfort, and ease of operation.

FIGURE 9-9
Zapf CRT/EDP station by Otto Zapf. Storage is now more efficient than ever with the addition of new horizontal paper management accessories for computer printouts or letter storage, stackable and interchangeable in overhead storage units. *Courtesy: Knoll International*

FIGURE 9-10

Boorum & Pease has developed a complete system of word processing modules that will handle any type of media that an office worker may use. Mini floppy, floppy disk and mag card trays are available and they may be housed in tray holders that also store soft copy; an efficiency file and spoked work organizer affords even tighter control over paper record management; and, a word processing cabinet holds all these units, allowing users to store all their media neatly, compactly and efficiently in one place. These components work with the user. It meets current demands and expands as these demands change and grow. The cabinet and tray holders can be mounted on the walls to accommodate a user with limited floor space. *Courtesy: Boorum & Pease Co.*

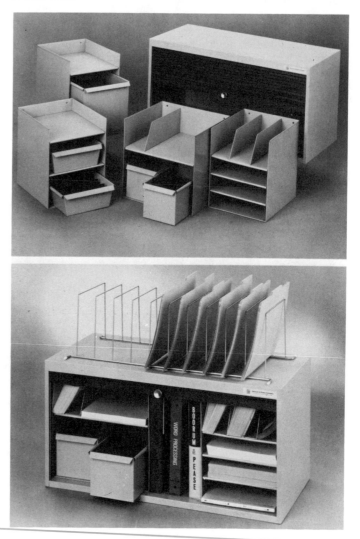

Tilt-Top CRT Turntables

In addition to offering workstation desks and components, special accessories include CRT turntables that tilt and turn for greater operator and machine productivity. Tilt-top turntables help reduce employee problems by making the operator more comfortable and improving CRT position within the workstation. Tilt-top turntables are recommended for use with CRT terminals having detachable keyboards. This allows a greater range of positions and versatility. (See Figures 9–11 to 9–14.)

FIGURE 9-11
Fits the CRT to the operator

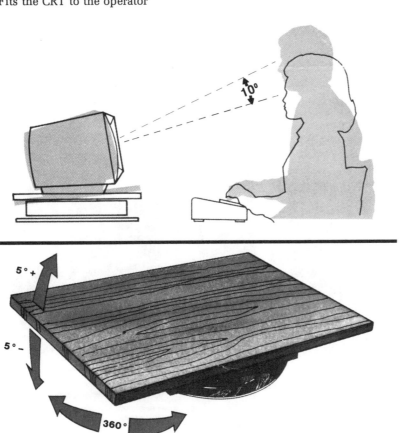

FIGURE 9-12
It tilts . . . It turns

FIGURE 9-13
Tilt/swivel accessory (right) is a feature on many systems.
Courtesy: Hewlett-Packard

FIGURE 9-14
Steelcase Ultronic 9000 VDT stand. *Courtesy: Steelcase*

What to Do About Wires and Cables

The electronic office may be a model of efficiency by using the latest hardware, but the more terminals and components are added to your office, the more wires and cables become a problem. *Wire management* is becoming one of the main problems for office designers. Every machine has an electrical wire or cable, and if there is no place to put these wires, there can be a tangle of them on the floor. This is unsightly, but even more important, it is unsafe.

Office furniture designers and manufacturers are trying to deal with this problem by running wires through a *raceway* (an open space) at the bottom of the landscape screens. The cables run through the raceway to a power pole or tube that carries the wires to electrical outlets, which may be located in the wall, ceiling, or floor, depending on the system. This plan keeps wires out of sight, off the floor, and eliminates a potential safety hazard.

171

FIGURE 9-15
To support the growing use of electronic equipment, Rosemount
has designed a simplified panel system that separates electrical
lines from communication cables. The communications raceway
is located at the bottom of each panel and can hold up to fourteen
25-pair cables, offering ample room for present needs and future
expansion. *Courtesy: Rosemount*

Cables and wires along the base of a floor can be
covered up with an attractive, adhesive insulator called CORD-COVER. The user can put CORD-COVER around
appliance cords, and firmly attach them to the floor
surface. It comes in 6-foot lengths, and a choice of
colors.

FIGURE 9-16
Cord-cover. *Courtesy: Winders & Geist*

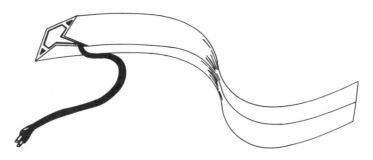

Seating

For maximum comfort and productivity, rotating worker assignments during the course of the day will give CRT terminal workers a break from sitting behind the terminal all day. Sitting, however, becomes critical if you work behind a word processor for any length of time. A well-designed chair with a firm back and good support will add to worker comfort.

FIGURE 9-17a
Since the Bio Chair has been designed around human factors as they relate to task operation in today's office, it is appropriate for use in conventional or open offices. *Courtesy: American Seating Co.*

FIGURE 9-17b
The Bio Chair complements open office systems. The functioning of this chair as an extension of the anatomy is a result of a natural evolution in seating. The result is that the most important element is the worker. *Courtesy: American Seating Co.*

Companies are now evaluating the seating accepted as the norm in today's working environment. The result of this effort is the development of a new seat—the Bio Chair™ developed by American Seating of Grand Rapids, Michigan. The Bio Chair has been designed to move with the occupant throughout his full range of daily activities. The chair takes on supportive action for many body motions: leaning forward while writing at a desk, erect while focusing on a CRT display, tilting back while in thought, conversation, stretching, or relaxing. The ability of the chair to move with the occupant is accomplished through these features:

1. *Back*—The back can be adjusted for preferred pitch. It can pivot and rotate simultaneously, accommodating shifts in body position and providing back support at all times and in all positions.

2. *Seat*—The molded seat cushion supports the body, and the soft waterfall perimeter of the seat extends the body weight to the legs without hindering circulation in the popliteal area behind the knees.

3. *Five Star Base*—For the ultimate in stability and safety, the five star base, with its abrasive-proof injection-molded plastic caps is a standard feature on the Bio Chair. Compared to the conventional four star base, it is less likely to tip.

4. *Seat-Height Adjustment*—Seat height can be controlled manually or automatically. Automatic adjustments in both seat height and back inclination are made by turning a single knob located on the right side of the seat. The knob can be reached easily from the sitting position. It is linked to a double-acting cam, which activates one or both of two pneumatic cylinders controlling changes in seat height and back inclination.

As the name suggests, the Bio Chair offers the word processing user a direct relationship between the chair and the human body. By meeting workers' postural requirements, this well designed chair works with the occupants to keep them alert, active, productive, and happy.

Steelcase incorporates an anthropometric design. Their chairs offer a "waterfall" front for reduced high-pressure and a posture-correct back design for reduced back strain in task intensive operations. Steelchase's ConCentrx operator's model features a posture back regulated by a rubber-packed spring. Back tension is adjusted by a T-handle located underneath the chair. Height adjustment is either manual or the touch-actuated pneumatic option featured on all ConCentrx chairs.

FIGURE 9-18
ConCentrx chairs. *Courtesy: Steelcase*

There has been much concern among workers that prolonged exposure to visual display terminals will lead to health problems. Many studies were initiated to determine whether these VDTs, which are fast becoming standard office tools, posed any radiation hazards to users. Most of the conclusions have re-

HEALTH AND SAFETY CONDITIONS

vealed that terminals emit only a very insignificant amount of radiation, certainly less than your home TV screens, and well below federal safety maximums. However, the study did uncover other health dangers that have the potential to cause long-term injury to regular VDT users, if certain precautionary measures are not taken.

The most common and potentially serious complaint is that of eye strain and other related visual problems. VDT operators who use the screens regularly report a range of troubles that include sore eyes, tearing, and an inability to focus. Although these may be temporary problems that do not lead to such long-term disabilities as permanent near-sightedness, chronic tendonitis, or arthritis, managers should be concerned because these problems are unpleasant to the workers on a day-to-day basis and obviously could affect worker performance and productivity. Some researchers feel that eye problems from prolonged use of VDTs occur because the cathode ray tubes create an image by repeatedly passing an electron beam across the screen. They speculate that the flicker caused by the beam painting a new picture 25 times or more a second, irritates the eye. To reduce some of these problems, the operator should adjust the screen's contrast, the position of the screen, and the position of the chair to get the best possible view.

The National Institute for Occupational Safety and Health (NIOSH) will continue to make studies and recommendations concerning potential health hazards in VDTs.

Word processing manufacturers are now designing equipment with the worker comfort and health factors in mind. The partnership of research efforts and investigations into this problem by government agencies, hardware manufacturers, private consultants, and professional associations[1] should be on-

---

[1]The Association of Information Systems Professionals (AISP) has published articles and studies relating to this problem in its magazine, *Words*. It has also presented sessions on operator safety and health during its Symposiums and Syntopicans. For more information, contact: Association of Information Systems Professionals (AISP), 1015 North York Road, Willow Grove, PA 19090.

going to investigate the broader concerns of health and safety factors.

"We should not just look at the eye but at the brain—the whole psychology" says IBM's Lewis M. Branscomb, Vice President and chief scientist at IBM, the leader of ergonomic design. "The heart of these issues is to understand what the person is trying to do, not just looking at the physical machine."[2] The following suggestions are offered to help operators deal with VDTs:

How to Avoid Mistakes in Operating Video Terminals[3]

- Give employees rest breaks, particularly heavy users.
- Buy movable keyboards and adjustable chairs.
- Add coatings, hoods, and other aids to reduce glare on the screen.
- Upgrade training programs to insure the proper use of equipment.
- Listen to employee complaints about working on the equipment.
- Don't place terminals adjacent to one another.
- Don't put a terminal next to a window or under high-intensity lighting.
- Require operators with bifocal glasses to have eye tests before working on VDTs.

Controlling Noise

In the electronic office, noise can be a contributing factor to the discomfort of workers. Although keyboarding on electronic word processors is virtually silent, the chief culprit is the printer.

[2]Reprinted from the June 30, 1980 issue of *Business Week* by special permission, © 1980 by McGraw-Hill, Inc., New York, N.Y. 10020. All rights reserved.
[3]Ibid.

In an office environment, noise is a serious problem because it lowers employee morale and efficiency. Noise interferes with communication and makes concentration exceedingly difficult and may result in irritation, nervousness, and headaches which lead to inefficiency and increased absenteeism.

Acoustical enclosures that fit over printers and other output devices can "quiet the storm." The box which houses the printer is made of wood and insulated by high-density, sound absorbent foam. A lid can be lifted to access the printer within; a fan inside the enclosure dissipates heat build-up.

Several manufacturers have designed unique and attractive sound controllers that will not interfere with efficiency. All keyboard, switches, controls are easily accessible and designs come in acrylic tops and are cantilevered to swing up easily and stay where they're put.

FIGURE 9-19
Jensen acoustical enclosure with engineered air vents to insure proper cooling. *Courtesy: Jensen Engineering*

FIGURE 9-20
The Jensen acoustical enclosure accommodates forms tractors.
Courtesy: Jensen Engineering

FIGURE 9-21
The Sound Controller, shown with Lanier system and Qume
printer, allows the use of tractor feeds. *Courtesy: Gates
Acoustinet, Inc.*

FIGURE 9-22
Typical Sound Controller used with printers with sheet feeders in place such as DT, Rutishauser or Datamarc. *Courtesy: Gates Acoustinet, Inc.*

One of the most efficient sound control systems has been designed by Jensen Engineering, Inc., of Santa Rosa, California. They have engineered their systems to provide more than 80-percent noise reduction on most office machines. Every Jensen enclosure contains vents, ducts and whisper fans to keep your equipment running at the proper temperature. (See Figures 9–19 and 9–20.)

The Future 10

As you read the pages of this book, you focus on a single technology—word processing—and a single tool—the word processor.

Historically, word processing and the word processor have been a discrete technology and a separate tool along with other components of office automation—facsimile devices, impact printers, copiers, and data processors. Today we are moving toward a holistic perspective and businesses are subscribing to a system integration philosophy where word, data, image, and voice processing are all bound together into a comprehensive office system. Analysts predict that word processing will increasingly join forces with the other technologies where word processing will form a generic interface for all text handling in integrated office systems.

The 1980s will be the critical decade for office automation planners. Strategists and corporate executives are making choices that may well determine our long-term future. We may not know the precise

FIGURE 10-1
The Wang audio workstation integrates Alliance support
functions, word processing, dictation, and voice messaging
functions. *Courtesy: Wang Laboratories*

nature of these choices, but futurists agree that our
actions today, tomorrow, next week, next month, and
next year will reverberate throughout the years ahead.

Certain trends have clearly emerged in word
processing. Systems are getting better and the potential for improving productivity is growing. One
example consists of sophisticated clustered workstations in which WP interacts with, rather than integrates, data processing. We are starting to build the
structure of the future office today. Although we are
not yet sure what form that structure will eventually
take, we do know that the computer will be the cor-
nerstone upon which it is built. The hardware is
available now: developments in software continue to
arrive.

Looking further into the future, many other key
office tasks will be facilitated by word processing
capabilities for managers and secretaries alike. Building upon the current array of word processors and
desktop computers, we will start with the familiar,
the proven, and move toward the sophisticated. The
future office is no one vendor's copyright. It is being
defined by those industries and professionals who are
paying the most attention to real-life office needs and
are innovating accordingly.

We must address some of these key issues: How

fast can office functions be moved into the interactive and communicating environments? How quickly will workers and managers adapt to these changes? Are those advanced changes really necessary for all office environments? Are we talking about large corporate structures only, and not about the two-to-ten person office or the single professional—the doctor, the attorney, the engineer, the author (see Figure 10–3) working at his or her terminal? Can special software be developed to meet the special needs of users and diverse applications? The word processing industry is in a transitional period about to enter yet another state of intense change.

Dataquest, the high technology market research subsidiary of A.C. Nielson Company, has collaborated with the editors of *Modern Office Procedures* magazine to present a special status report on the emerging trends in the word processing industry.

FIGURE 10-2
Office automation systems. *Courtesy: Honeywell*

FIGURE 10-3
A typical workstation. *Courtesy: Honeywell*

Following are some of the highlights of this White Paper Report, "Word Processing in Transition."[1]

Between 1981 and 1986, the U.S. market for word processing workstations will continue to expand. Although deliveries should increase at a compound annual growth rate of 27 percent during this period, it is a slower percentage growth rate than the 33 percent growth of the 1976–81 period. In actual units we believe that approximately 214,000 units were shipped in 1981 and that 718,000 units will be shipped in 1986. The projected slowdown in growth rate is related to two factors:

- The $5,000 to $15,000 pure word processing workstations will have penetrated 30 percent of the U.S. heavy duty typewriter installed base by 1986, and that is a projected saturation point.

- The transitional effect of universal workstations that do everything will make it possible to call a product a word processor per

[1]Lindsey, Clifford, and Robert Costain, "White Paper Report: Word Processing in Transition," *Modern Office Procedures* (June 1982), pp. 51–60.

se. We believe that many different devices

will satisfy the typing needs of the United
States in 1986.

Workstation Configuration

Workstations can be classified in one dimension
as having a certain display-size characteristic,
and in the other dimension as stand-alone or
clusterable (i.e., a configuration characteristic).
Table 10–1 estimates the overall workstation
market when segmented on a configuration
basis:

FIGURE 10-4
Fortune Systems' 32:16 can handle the requirements of a one
person office. Or it can expand to a complete system for a small to
medium-sized business or a department of a large corporation.
Courtesy: Fortune Systems

TABLE 10-1
United States WP Workstations

DELIVERIES (K)				
	1981		1986	
	UNITS	%	UNITS	%
STANDALONE	55.3	26%	97.0	13%
CLUSTER	158.6	74%	621.1	87%
TOTAL	213.9	100%	718.1	100%

STANDALONE DELIVERIES (K)				
	1981		1986	
	UNITS	%	UNITS	%
STANDALONE (NON-CLUSTERABLE)	55.3	37%	97.0	21%
STANDALONE (CLUSTERABLE)	93.4	63%	372.5	79%
TOTAL STANDALONE	148.7	100%	469.5	100%

CLUSTER SEGMENT DELIVERIES (K)				
	1981		1986	
	UNITS	%	UNITS	%
INDEPENDENT CLUSTER	93.4	59%	372.5	60%
DEPENDENT CLUSTER	65.2	41%	248.6	40%
TOTAL CLUSTER	158.6	100%	621.1	100%

Courtesy: Dataquest and *Modern Office Procedures*

SUMMARY OF TRENDS AND WHAT DOES ALL THIS MEAN?

Shakespeare's Hamlet may have been pondering that question when he said, "Suit the action to the word, the word to the action." The word processing industry is in a period of rapid change, and each of us must step lively to avoid being left behind. Dataquest concludes this comprehensive report and suggests expectations for three primary groups within the office automation family—vendors, office executives, and equipment users. The following are Dataquest's conclusions for equipment users—the primary readers of this book:

- Expect less tedium in performing repetitive or mechanical functions.
- Anticipate more assistance with remembering things and finding information.
- Look forward to organizing tasks more readily.
- Look forward to going to work on Monday morn-

ing because the office will be less frustrating and more *fun*.

The Future

- Expect the new office machines to be your electronic servants. You will not service the machine; the machine will enhance your creativity, intellect, and effectiveness.[2]

Individual reprints of this White Paper are available in its entirety. They are bound in a clear plastic cover. Price is $3. Please specify the title, "Word Processing in Transition" June, 1982. Please send your order and check to: Reprint Editor, *Modern Office Procedures,* 1111 Chester Avenue, Cleveland, Ohio 44114.

AND FINALLY . . . A LOOK AT THE 21ST CENTURY: WORD PROCESSING AND BEYOND

We are on the threshold of a new era. The year 2000 is approaching. What will life be like in the new century? It will be as different as the way we live today compared with the way we lived in the 1940s.

Imagine yourself in the year 2000. The forecasts say that you, as an average American, will have an income of some $70,000 a year. You'll drive a $30,000 car that gets almost 50 miles to the gallon of gas. When you go to the supermarket, you'll find that food will take a three-times-larger share of your paycheck than it does today. So, you'll be eating less meat, and more non-meat protein. You'll have only two children, instead of today's three. And, you'll probably be living in an apartment or townhouse, not a conventional home. More and more of you will be moving to southern and western states. You'll create new jobs, new communities, and new lifestyles.

Scenario of an Electric Word Odyssey

You will awake on a February morning in the year 2002, go for a swim in your pool, and then return to your New Mexico townhouse for breakfast and a full

---

[2]Ibid.

FIGURE 10-5
Western Union's Westar IV and V. *Courtesy: Western Union*

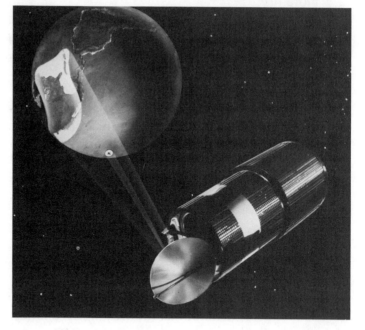

day's work in the office. After pouring yourself a glass of orange juice, you turn on your terminal to scan the *Wall Street Journal*. Each page appears clearly, beamed from a satellite. As you depress other keys, another page appears on the screen. You come across an item of interest and depress a third key which allows you to store the page in one of several banks you use in your business.

Your office is down the hall from your kitchen. The room itself is quite similar to those of the mid-twentieth century—lined with oak bookshelves on the wall and a large gleaming desk. A bank of micro-computers sit atop the back of the desk. These replace the usual in-and-out baskets and stacks of paper by informing you, at the push of a button, of your schedule for time ahead, business of the day, and whatever other data you may wish to review. At one end, facing the desk, is the key to the office of the future—a video camera trained on the chair in which you sit.

You begin your work by dictating several letters. You speak quickly into the microphone, not at all normally, stressing some syllables and pronouncing a

FIGURE 10-6
A future "home-office"

few words differently than they would sound in ordinary conversation. The words appear on your video display terminal the instant they are uttered. *This is your voice recognition terminal in action!* No secretary or typist is needed as you bypass the keyboarding and transcribing tasks. Your words appear correct after you have reviewed them on the screen, and then you send them out over your telephone line to come out in the storage unit of the person you are communicating with.

Now you turn your attention to a meeting in New York. With a few pushes of buttons on your terminal, there appears on the screen an image of your associates in corporate headquarters in a Video Conference Center in New York. You discuss your business deals via audio and video connection. Occasionally charts and diagrams appear on the screen, with copies instantly being transmitted when needed. Once, when verification of a particular point was needed, you put New York "on hold," called a banker in London and asked him to send documents to corporate headquarters in New York.

One of the New York corporate staff wants to give a contract to the Silver Construction Company in New Zealand. As he speaks, you press more terminal keys, and out comes a credit report for the company indicating it is a good risk. You sign off, then call Aukland. After a few minutes, it is clear the contact there had done some verification of his own.

Then each person calls lawyers—one in Los Angeles, the other in Tokyo—leaving the details to these two, who will call one another several times during the next two days.

To celebrate the deal, you and the representative of the Silver Construction Company go to lunch—electronically. You insist on paying. You press a few buttons, and within less than a minute each person has been provided with a menu on each terminal. Yours from a little restaurant in Santa Fe and your guest's from a restaurant in Aukland. All of this is done electronically, as were the orders. The meals arrive a half-hour later by messenger, including wines and desserts. You enjoy your lunch and conclude by toasting one another as you view each other over your video screens.

That afternoon begins with another brief swim, and follows with additional correspondence and calls. In the evening, you relax by taking an electronic stroll through New York City. Moving a lever, you advance northward up Madison Avenue, moving your lever which activates a camera to give you sweeping views or close-ups of the shops and boutiques along Madison Avenue. You turn your lever at 82 Street toward the Metropolitan Museum. Every street in New York was programmed into the city—or a selection of cities on your tour library.

Can this story ever become a reality? Even though this scenario might seem like fiction, some of the technology already exists. It will soon be available. Of course, new discoveries will be made to make this scenario even more inviting and life more interesting. These systems are merely forerunners of the new "knowledge engineering" industry that has the power to transform every layer of society.

Word processing—the technology and the machine—as part of the large umbrella of information technology, is a game in which every player can win. To businesses, large and small, it holds out opportunities for huge gains in productivity. For individuals, it can make possible improvements in the quality of both their personal and professional working lives.

Appendix

This list includes companies identified as manufacturing and selling word and information systems and terminals, both stand-alone and shared systems. It also includes companies that sell and manufacture personal computers and/or microprocessors capable of word processing functions and applications.

AB DICK COMPANY
5700 West Touhy
Chicago, IL 60648

ADLER-ROYAL BUSINESS
MACHINES
1600 Route 22
Union City, NJ 07083

AES DATA
570 McCaffrey Street
Montreal, CANADA H4T 1N1

ALTOS COMPUTER
SYSTEMS
2338 A Walsh Avenue
Santa Clara, CA 95050

APPLE COMPUTER, INC.
10260 Bandley Drive
Cupertino, CA 95014

ATARI INC.
1265 Borregas Avenue
P.O. Box 9027
Sunnyvale, CA 94086

ATV JACQUARD, INC.
2921 South Damier
Santa Ana, CA 92711

AXXA
21201 Oxnard Street
Woodland Hills, CA 91367

**WORD PROCESSING
SYSTEMS VENDORS**

193

BASIC/FOUR
CORPORATION
14101 Myford Road
Tustin, CA 92680

BURROUGHS
CORPORATION
30 Main Street
Danbury, CT 06810

CADO SYSTEMS
CORPORATION
2771 Toledo Street
Torrance, CA 90503

COMMODORE BUSINESS
MACHINES
Valley Force Corporate Center
950 Rittenhouse Road
Norristown, PA 19403

COMPAL, INC.
6300 Variel Avenue
Woodland Hills, CA 91367

COMPUCORP
1901 S. Bundy Drive
Los Angeles, CA 90025

CONVERGENT
TECHNOLOGIES
2500 Augustine Drive
Santa Clara, CA 95051

CPT
8100 Mitchell Road
Minneapolis, MN 90404

DATA GENERAL
CORPORATION
15 Turnpike Road
Westboro, MA 01581

DATAPOINT
CORPORATION
9725 Datapoint Drive
San Antonio, TX 78284

DICTAPHONE
CORPORATION
120 Old Post Road
Rye, NY 10580

DIGITAL EQUIPMENT
CORPORATION
146 Main Street
Maynard, MA 01754

EXXON OFFICE SYSTEMS
Long Ridge Road
Stanford, CT 06904

FORTUNE SYSTEMS
CORPORATION
1501 Industrial Road
San Carlos, CA 94070

FOUR-PHASE SYSTEMS,
INC.
10700 N. de Anza Blvd.
Cupertino, CA 95014

FRANKLIN COMPUTER
CORP.
7030 Colonial Highway
Pennsauken, NJ 08109

GRID SYSTEMS
2535 Garcia Ave.
Mountain View, CA 94943

HEWLETT-PACKARD
GSD Division
19447 Prunridge Avenue
Cupertino, CA 95014

HONEYWELL
INFORMATION SYSTEMS
200 Smith Street
Waltham, MA 01821

IBM CORPORATION
National Accounts Division
600 Mamaroneck Avenue
Harrison, NY 10528

KAY COMPUTERS DIV.
Nonlinear Systems
533 Stevens Avenue
Solana Beach, CA 92075

LANIER BUSINESS
PRODUCTS
1700 Chantilly Drive, NE
Atlanta, GA 30324

MITEL CORP.
Office Products Div.
302 Legget Drive
Kanata, Ont. Can. KZK 1Y6

MOHAWK DATA SYSTEM
Seven Century Drive
Parsippany, NJ 07054

NBI, INC.
P.O. Box 9001
1695 38th Street
Boulder, CO 80301

NCR CORPORATION
1700 South Patterson Blvd.
Dayton, OH 45479

NEC INFORMATION
SYSTEMS, INC.
5 Militia Drive
Lexington, MA 02173

NIXDORF COMPUTER
CORPORATION
300 Third Avenue
Waltham, MA 02154

NORTHERN TELECOM
SYSTEMS CORPORATION
Electronic Office Systems
P.O. Box 1222
Data Park
Minneapolis, MN 55440

NORTH STAR COMPUTER,
INC.
14440 Cataline Street
San Leandro, CA 94577

OHIO SCIENTIFIC, INC.
1333 S. Chillicothe Road
Aurora, OH 44202

OLIVETTI CORPORATION
OF AMERICA
155 White Plains Road
Tarrytown, NY 10591

OLYMPIA USA, INC.
Box 22
Somerville, NJ 08876

OSBORNE COMPUTER
CORP.
26500 Corporate Ave.
Haywood, CA 94545

PHILIPS INFORMATION
SYSTEMS, INC.
4040 McEwen
Dallas, TX 75234

RADIO SHACK/TANDY
CORP.
1300 One Tandy Center
Fort Worth, TX 76102

RAYTHEON DATA
SYSTEMS
1415 Boston-Providence
Turnpike
Norwood, MA 02062

ROYAL BUSINESS
MACHINES
150 New Park Avenue
Hartford, CT 06106

SANYO BUSINESS
EQUIPMENT
51 Joseph Street
Moonachie, NJ 07074

SILICON VALLEY
SYSTEMS, INC.
1625 El Camino Real #4
Belmont, CA 94002

SINCLAIR RESEARCH LTD.
One Sinclair Plaza
Nashua, NH 03061

SONY CORPORATION OF
AMERICA
Office Products Division
9 West 57 Street
New York, NY 10019

SYNTREX, INC.
246 Industrial Way West
Eatontown, NJ 07724

SYSTEL
538 Oakmead Pkwy
Sunnyvale, CA 94086

TEC, INC.
2727 N. Fairview Ave.
P.O. Box 5646
Tucson, AZ 85703

TEXAS INSTRUMENTS,
INC.
P.O. Box 202146
Dallas, TX 75220

3M
3M Center
St. Paul, MN 55101

TOSHIBA AMERICA, INC.
Information Processing
Division
2441 Michelle Drive
Tustin, CA 92680

VECTOR GRAPHIC, INC.
500 North Ventu Park Road
Thousand Oaks, CA 91320

VICTOR BUSINESS
PRODUCTS
P.O. Box 1135
Glenview, IL 60025

WANG LABORATORIES,
INC.
1 Industrial Avenue
Lowell, MA 01851

WORDPLEX
141 Triunfo Canyon Road
Westlake Village, CA 91381

XEROX CORPORATION
Office Products Division
1341 West Mockingbird Lane
Dallas, TX 75247

ZENITH DATA SYSTEM
1000 Milwaukee Avenue
Glenview, IL 60025

WORD PROCESSING SUPPLIES (RIBBONS, PRINTWHEELS, MAGNETIC MEDIA)

AGT COMPUTER
PRODUCTS, INC.
3701 Highland Avenue
Manhattan Beach, CA 90266

AMPEX BUSINESS
PRODUCTS
Division of Ampex Corp.
1615 Prudential
Dallas, TX 75235

APD BUSINESS MACHINES
10717 Camino Ruiz
San Diego, CA 92126

ASPEN RIBBONS, INC.
1700 North 55th Street
Boulder, CO 87030

BASF SYSTEMS
Business Products Group
Crosby Drive
Bedford, MA 01730

BOORUM & PEASE
Vernon McMilan
801 Newark Avenue
Elizabeth, NJ 07208

BUD INFORMATION
SYSTEMS
Division of Tesco, Inc.
1931 Greenspring Drive
Timonium, MD 21093

CAMWIL, INC.
875 Waemanu Street
Honolulu, Hawaii 96813

COLUMBIA GREAT LAKES
CORP.
35 South Street Clare Street
Dayton, OH 45402

COLUMBIA RIBBON &
CARBON
MFG CO., INC.
P.O. Box 1629
Union City, NJ 07083

COMPT-TYPE BUSINESS
PRODUCTS
4620 Manilla Road, S.E.
Calgary, Alberta CANADA
T27 4B7

COOPER COPY CO., INC.
365 Glenwood Drive
East Orange, NJ 07017

COPY CRAFT
CORPORATION
P.O. Box 5044-396
2505 Thousand Oaks Blvd
Thousand Oaks, CA 91359

DAISY WHEEL RIBBON CO.,
INC.
9375 Archibald Avenue
Cucamonga, CA 91730

DATA EXCHANGE, INC.
36 Cherry Lane
Floral Park, NY 11001

DATAPRODUCTS
CORPORATION
6200 Canoga Avenue
Woodland Hills, CA 91365

DENNISON KYBE
CORPORATION
82 Calvary Street
Waltham, MA 02254

DENNISON NATIONAL
Subsidiary of Dennison Mfg.
Co.
Water Street
Holyoke, MA 01040

DIABLO SYSTEMS, INC.
24500 Industrial Blvd.
Hayward, CA 94545

DYSAN CORP.
5201 Patrick Henry Drive
Santa Clara, CA 95050

EASTERN SPECIALITIES
CO., INC.
287 Northfield Road
P.O. Box N181
Northfield, IL 60093

E.D. POE ASSOCIATES
941 Westwood Blvd.
Los Angeles, CA 90024

EICHNER SYSTEMS, INC.
1460 Industrial Drive
Itasca, IL 60143

ESSELTE PENDAFLEX
CORP
Clinton Road
Garden City, NY 11530

GRAHAM MAGNETICS
1200 Summit Avenue
Ft. Worth, TX 76194

INFO TECH
36 Cherry Lane
Floral Park, NY 11001

INMAC
2645 Augustine Drive
Santa Clara, CA 95051

INTERNATIONAL
BUSINESS SUPPLIES, INC.
P.O. Box 742
Brentwood, TN 37027

LEADING EDGE PRODUCTS,
INC
222 Turnpike St.
Canton, MA 02021

MAGNETIC
TECHNOLOGIES, INC.
One Fulton Ave.
Hempstead, NY 11550

MAXELL CORPORATION
60 Oxford Drive
Moonachie, NJ 07074

MEMOREX D.I.C.
CORPORATION
P.O. Box 900
1200 Memorex Drive
Santa Clara, CA 95052

NASHUA CORPORATION
44 Franklin Street
Nashua, NH 03060

OFFICE PRODUCTS
INTERNATIONAL
P.O. Box 26399
Denver, CO 80226

OMNI RESOURCES
4 Oak Pound Ave.
Millbury, MA 01527

OPTIMUM TESTED
PRODUCTS, INC.
30 Jefryn Blvd. West
Deer Park, NY 11729

PAN AMERICAN BUSINESS
SYSTEMS
130 Novner Drive
Cincinnati, OH 45215

QUIET DESIGNS, INC.
473 Macara Avenue
Sunnyvale, CA 94086

QUME CORPORATION
2350 Qume Drive
San Jose, CA 95131

ROYAL BUSINESS
MACHINES, INC.
150 New Park Avenue
Hartford, CT 06106

SMOKEY MOUNTAIN
RIBBON & SUPPLY, INC.
P.O. Box 742
Brentwood, TN 37027

SUPER OFFICE STORE
P.O. Box 457
15305 Box 457
15305 Midway Road
Addison, TX 75001

SYNCOM
P.O. Box 130
Mitchell, SD 57301

THIRD WAVE PRODUCTS
2 Pequot Park
Canton, MA 02021

3M COMPANY
Data Recording Products Div.
223-5N 3M Center
St. Paul, MN 55144

TYPERITE RIBBON MFG.
INC.
38-04 48th Street
Long Island City, NY 11104

UARCO, INC.
West County Line Road
Barrington, IL 60010

VERBATIM
323 Soquel Way
Sunnyvale, CA 94086

VISTA INFORMATION
PRODUCTS
1540 E. Edinger Avenue
Santa Ana, CA 92705

WABASH TAPE
CORPORATION
Two Continental Towers
1701 Golf Road
Rolling Meadows, IL 60008

WILSON JONES COMPANY
5150 W. Touhy Avenue
Chicago, IL 60648

WORD ALGEBRA, INC.
223 West Hubbard Street
Chicago, IL 60610

WORDEX CORPORATION
1965 Adams Avenue
San Leandro, CA 94577

RESOURCES FOR CURRENT READING

Magazines

BYTE - THE SMALL
SYSTEMS JOURNAL
70 Main Street
Peterborough, NH 03458

CANADIAN OFFICE
Whitsed Publishing
55 Bloor Street
Toronto, Ontario CANADA
M4W 3M1

COMPUTER DECISIONS
Hayden Publishing Data
Center
50 Essex Street
Rochelle Park, NJ 07662

CREATIVE COMPUTING
P.O. Box 789-M
Morristown, NJ 07960

DATA COMMUNICATIONS
McGraw-Hill Inc.
1221 Avenue of the Americas
New York, NY 10020

DATAMATION
Technical Publishing
1301 S. Grove Avenue
Barrington, IL 60010

DM - DATA MANAGEMENT
Data Processing Management
Assoc. (DPMA)
505 Busse Highway
Park Ridge, IL 60068

INFORMATION & RECORDS
MANAGEMENT
250 Fulton Avenue
Hempstead, NY 11550

HIGH TECHNOLOGY
38 Commercial Warf
Boston, MA 02110

INFOSYSTEMS
Hitchcock Publishing Co.
Hitchcock Bldg.
Wheaton, IL 60187

INTERACTIVE COMPUTING
Assoc. of Computer Users
P.O. Box 9003
Boulder, CO 80301

JOURNAL OF SYSTEMS
MANAGEMENT
Association for Systems
Management
24587 Bagley Road
Cleveland, OH 44138

LE BUREAU
Maclean-Hunter Limited
481 University Avenue
Toronto

MANAGEMENT WORLD
Administrative Management
Society (AMS)
2360 Maryland Road
Willow Grove, PA 19090

MODERN OFFICE
PROCEDURES
P.O. Box 95759
Cleveland, OH 44101

OFFICE ADMINISTRATION
AND AUTOMATION
Geyer-McAllister
Publications
51 Madison Avenue
New York, NY 10010

OFFICE EQUIPMENTS &
METHODS
Maclean-Hunter Limited
481 University Avenue
Toronto, Ontario
CANADA m5W 1A7

THE OFFICE
Office Publications Inc
1200 Summer Street
Stamford, CT 06904

onCOMPUTING
onCOMPUTING, INC.
70 Main Street
Peterborough, NH 03458

PERSONAL COMPUTING
P.O. Box 2941
Boulder, CO 80321

THE SECRETARY
Professional Secretary's
International (PSI)
2440 Pershing Road
Kansas City, MO 64108

TODAY'S OFFICE
Hearst Business
Communications
UTP Division
645 Stewart Avenue
Garden City, NY 11530

WORDS
AISP
1015 North York Road
Willow Grove, PA 19090

ADVANCED OFFICE
CONCEPTS
One Bala Cynwyd Plaza
Bala Cynwyd, PA 19004

CONSULTECH
Inst. for Mgt.
Development
The Guilford, Suite R
Sentry Place
Scarsdale, NY 10583

DUFFY & BENTLEY REPORT
Suite 202
663 Yonge Street
Toronto, Ontario
M4Y 2A4 CANADA

ELECTRONIC MAIL &
MESSAGE SYSTEMS
Int'l Resource Development
30 High Street
Norwalk, CT 06851

THE ERGONOMICS
NEWSLETTER
1301 Lachman Lane
Pacific Palisades, CA 90272

IMPACT: INFORMATION
TECHNOLOGY
Administrative Management
Society
2360 Maryland Road
Willow Grove, PA 19090

INFORMATION INDUSTRY
REVIEW (IIR)
AISP
1015 North York Road
Willow Grove, PA 19090

INFORMATION
MANAGEMENT
Center for Management
Systems
Box 3414
Sioux City, IA 51102

INFORMATION & WORD
PROCESSING REPORT
Geyer McAllister
Publications
51 Madison Avenue
New York, NY 10010

INSIDE WORD PROCESSING
Buyers Laboratory, Inc.
20 Railroad Avenue
Hackensack, NJ 07601

INTERCOMM
AISP
1015 North York Road
Willow Grove, PA 19090

OFFICEMATION PRODUCT
REPORTS
Management Information
Corporation
140 Barclay Center
Cherry Hill, NJ 08034

ONLINE DATABASE
REPORT
Link Resources Corp.
Subsidiary of International
Data Corporation
215 Park Avenue South
New York, NY 10003

THE OFFICE
PROFESSIONAL
116 E. Main Street
Round Rock, TX 78614

OPEN SYSTEMS
P.O. Box 1231
Stamford, CT 06904

SEYBOLD REPORT ON
OFFICE SYSTEMS
Seybold Publications, Inc.
Suite 801
44 Bromfield
Boston, MA 02108

THOMCOMP WORD
PROCESSING REPORT
P.O. Box 324
Double Bay, N.S.W. 2028
Australia

WORD PROCESSING
SECTION NEWSLETTER
Association of Computer
Users
P.O. Box 9003
Boulder, CO 80301

VIDEOPRINT
30 High Street
Norwalk, CT 06851

Index

A

accessories, 139
acoustic couplers, 104
acoustical enclosures, 178
Advanced Information Systems (AIS)
    Net 1 Service, 101
Advanced Micro Devices' 16-bit bipolar
    microprocessor, 19
Advanced Office Concepts Corp., 21, 84
agribusiness applications, 106
American Bell, 101
American Medical Association, 107
Anchor dot, 134
Anchor Pad International, Inc., 134
antistatic carpeting, 129
antistatic chairs, 130
Apple Computer, 46
applications programs, 46
Asimov, Isaac, 78

Association of Information Systems
    Professionals (AISP), 176
Automated Language Processing
    Systems (ALSP), 115

B

back-up systems, 137
banking applications, 68
banking correspondence, 68
Barkey, Ltd., 113
BASIC language, 88
bidirectional printers, 16
Bio Chair™, 174
black boxes, 103
Borum & Pease modules, 168
Branscomb, Lewis, 177

buck-slip, electronic, 97
buffer memory, 16, 18
bulletin boards, electronic, 117
bursters, 152

CRT workstations (See workstations, CRT)
cursor control keys, 25
cursors, 25, 27, 28, 34

C

Cancel Key, 28
Carter, Jimmy, 75
cathode rag tube (See workstations, CRT)
centering, automatic, 31
central processing unit (See CPU)
chairs, 173
character printers, high-speed, 7
character spacing, 46
characters, boldface, 33
Cerf, Christopher, 76
chips, 6, 18
coding instructions, 18
coding procedures, 24
columnar formats, 31
commands, 17
communications capability, 95
Compu-Chair, 130
Compucorp word processor, 45
CompuServe, 107
Computer Decisions, 83
computers, desktop, 5, 9
  software for, 46
computers, personal, 9, 11
computers, prices of, 9, 12
ConCentrx chairs, 175
Condon, Richard, 74
controls, brightness and contrast, 162
cord-covers, 172
CP/M 86, 47
CP/M operating system, 44, 47, 48
CPT, 47
CPT 8500 series, 165
CPU, 7, 8, 13, 131
Crichton, Michael, 74

D

daisy wheel printers, 14, 15, 132
Data Bank Subscription Services, 107
data banks, individualized, 77
data bases, 106
data processing, 9, 88
Dataguest, 183
decimal alignment, automatic, 31
delete function, 26
Delete key, 26
Derick, Bo, 75
desktop machines (See computers, desktop)
DEST Workless station, 97
diagnostics, 120
Dictaphone System 6000, 12, 40
dictionaries, customized, 44
Digital Research Corporation, 47
directional arrows, 25
disintegrators, 153
disk drives, 18
disk drives, Winchester, 18, 146
diskettes, (See floppy disks)
display systems, 6, 8
document:
  archiving, 7
  printing, 23
  production, 23
  revision, 23
  storage, 13
documents, medical, 73
dot-matrix printers (See matrix printers)
Dow Jones News Retrieval "A Service," 107
Dow Jones News Retrieval "B Service."
DP/WP multifunctional capabilities, 88

E

editability, 105
editing, 26
educational applications, 76
EIES Network, 107
Eisenberg, Robert S., 76
electric power surges, 131
electronic file cabinet, 90
Elkin, Stanley, 74
Envax 500, 104
envelope feeders, automatic, 151
ergonomics, 157
Escape Key, 28
Ethernet, 101

F

feeders, 151
Fiber optics, 15
file management, 52 (See also software features)
filters, 161
flexible disks (See floppy disks)
floppy disks, 17, 18, 20, 37, 89, 146
  filing, 146
  identifying, 149
  storage of, 126
footers, automatic, 52
footnoting, automatic, 32
footrests, 155
form letters, creation of, 53
form letters, personalized, 31
format functions, 18
format lines, 163
format storage, 28
  line spacing, 28
  margins, 28
  paragraph indentions, 28
  tab setting, 28
forms, business, 60

forms creation (See software features)
formulas, multilevel, 61
Fortune Systems' 32:16, 185

G

global replace feature, 32
glossary function (See software features)
graphics, 16, 21 (See also software features)

H

Hand disks (See Rigid disks)
hardware, 20
head cleaning, 127
headers, automatic, 52
health conditions, 175
Help functions, 27
Hendrix Teletypereader OCR system, 100
Herbert, Ernest, 74
Hersey, John, 74
Hewlett-Packard HP 125 Computer System, 10
Hewlett-Packard micro-floppy disks, 146
hyphenation, automatic, 31

I

IBM Displaywriter, 47, 75, 79
IBM's Selectric metal ball, 14

information bank services, 107
information banks, electronic, 105
information retrieval (See software
    features)
Inmac, 143
insert mode, 27
Insert Keys, 27
insertions, 27
Inside Word Processing, 82, 84
integrated information system, 87
Intel 2732, 19
interfaces, 104
internal memory, 18

Lanier, 47
    EX-1, 89
    No-Problem processor, 75
laser printing, 15, 147
legal applications, 71, 79–81, 106
letter quality printers, 15, 72
letters, individualized, 56
Lexis, 72, 108
Lifeboat Associates, 48
lighting, 161
line printers, 15, 22
list processing, 58 (See also software
    features)

J

Jensen acoustical enclosure, 178
Job, Steven, 46
Juris, 72
justification, 33

K

Kavanan, Louis, 132
key word indexing, automatic, 91
keyboard, QWERTY, 24
keyboarding, 23, 24, 25, 26, 164
keyboards, 12, 16, 24, 164
Kirk, John, 82

L

Labomatic chairs, 173
Language processing systems, 115

M

magnetic tapes, 19
mail:
    electronic, 85, 96, 107
    voice, 114
mailing lists, assembling, 31
maintenance, 119
    electrical power, 122
    external surfaces, 122
    floppy disks, 124
    keyboard, 122
    printer, 123, 131
    printwheel, 123, 132
    screen, 124
Management Contents, 107
mass mailings, creation of, 53
math packages (See software features)
matrix printers, 15, 16, 72
MCS photocomposition system, 95
medical applications, 30, 72, 106
memory, 18
memory chips (See chips)
merge feature, 33
merging, 53
Metpath, 108
microcomputers, business, 9, 46
microprocessors, 13, 19

minicomputers, 9
MnemoDisc™, 148
modems, 8, 95, 104, 117
modules, 20
move function, 28
multifunctional system (See terminals, multifunctional)
multisystem configuration, 90

N

NBI system 3000, 13
networks, telecommunications, 101
newsletters, electronic, 108
News Net, 108
Next Page function
Next Screen function, 27
Nixdorf, 6
noise, control of, 177
number alignment, automatic, 31

O

office of the future, 87, 181
OFIS reader 1240 OCR page reader, 100
Olivetti M-20, 65
Oops Key, 28
operating systems, 47
operating systems, CPM, 47
operational problems, 136
operator's manual, 120, 132
optical character recognition (OCR), 97, 117
optical disks, 146

P

Page Break command, 35
page reader, 98
page scanners, 98

pagination:
    automatic, 35
    manual, 34
paper shredders, 152
paragraphs, standard, 56
password protection, 45
Peachtree Software, 48
peripherals, 5, 104
Philips Micom 3003
Philips Micom's 2000/1, 8
phototypesetting, 91
phrase storage feature, 29, 30
Polaroid's CP-70 filter, 160
port extenders, 105
printers, 14, 15
printers, malfunction of, 121
printwheel applications, 144
printwheels, 143
processors, on-line, 19
prompt, 52, 120, 143
protocol translators, 104
proofreading, 17, 27
programs, 20
proportional printing (See software features)

Q, R

Quadex Composition Systems, 92
Radio Shack:
    TRS 80 line printer Model V, 16
    TRS-80 Model II, 78
    TRS Line Printer VIII, 16
    Videotex™ information retrieval system, 109
read-only memory (See ROM)
records management, 21, 89 (See also software features)
reports, printing, 51
return keys, 25
ribbon cartridges, 144
rigid disks, 18, 89

ROM, 19, 20
Rosemount panel system, 172

S

safety conditions, 175
Satellite Data Corporation, 113
satellite transmission, 112
scientific typing, 61
screens, 12
screens, glare-resistant, 159
Scripsit processor, 78
scrolling, 26, 27
search replace feature, 32
seating (See chairs)
security, 134
security racks, 134
security systems (See software features)
servicing policy, 135
Seward, Robert, 79
sheet feeders, automatic, 151
Shugart's SA 600, 18
silicon chip (See chips)
Smith-Corona TP-1 printer, 15
software, 20, 37–49
software, combination packages, 49
software features:
    file management, 39
    forms creation, 40
    glossary function, 29, 30, 44, 56, 58
    graphics, 40, 42, 63
    information retrieval, 40
    list processing, 38
    math packages, 38, 61
    proportional printing, 46
    records management, 39
    security systems, 45
    sorting, 40, 59
    spelling checking program, 44, 71
software, off-the-shelf, 48
software, programmable, 21
sound controllers, 178

Sorcim Corporation, 48
sorting (See software features)
spelling checking program (See
    software features)
Spell-Star Dictionary Software
    Program, 44
Spellwriter, 44
Sprint 9 printer, 14
static control floor mats, 129
static-controlled floor coverings, 130
staticstop, 129
status lines (See prompts)
Steelcase Ultronic 9000 VDT stand, 171
storage, media, 17, 18
subscripts, 34
SuperCalc² Electronic Worksheet, 48
superscripts, 34
suppliers, 140
supplies, 139
supplies, shelf life of, 127
systems:
    shared, 6, 7, 8
    stand-alone, 6, 8

T, U, V

telecommuting, 110
Telenet, 107
Telestaff, 111
Telex network, 104
terminals:
    multifunctional, 6, 9, 88
    single, 88
    telecopier, 96
    workstation, 13, 99
thimble print element, 14
Toffler, Alvin, 77, 110
Tower, Guy, 78
tractors, 152
trends, 183
turntables, CRT, 169
TWX networks, 104

typewriters:
   electronic, 5, 6, 18
   magnetic tape, 5
underscoring, automatic, 31
Undo functions, 27
Undo key, 28
Varityper's Comp/Set, 95
vendors, 9, 137
video conference center, 189
video screen displays, 48
voice mail, 114
voice recognition terminal, 189
voice stored-and-forward processing,
   111
Voltector Series 6 AC Power
   Conditioner, 130

Welch, Raquel, 75
Western Union's Westar IV and V, 188
Westlaw, 72
window command, 65
wires, 171
Wohl, Amy, 21, 84, 105
word processing, definition of, 5
"Word Processing in Transition," 184
word processing systems,
   manufacturers of, 6
word processors, maintenance of (See
   maintenance)
Words, 176
Wordstar, 48
workstation configurations, 186
workstation terminals (See terminals,
   workstation)
workstations, CRT, 7, 8, 12, 13, 167, 182
wraparound feature, 25
wrist support platforms, 154

W

wafers, 20
Wang:
   audio workstation, 182
   Professional Computer, 113
Wangnet, 101
Wangwriter, 47

X, Y, Z

The Yankee Group, 107
Zapf CRT/EDP workstation, 167
Ziyad Z-3000 paper processor, 151